Invitation to Partner in

Project

Beloved in Christ,

The Restoration House is a prayer altar for the nations.
By God's faithfulness and your sacrificial support, we secured 1,000 m² of land (30 million FCFA / $54,000) in 2022. Since then, 34 million FCFA ($60,200) has been invested in documents, site preparation, and the foundation. May God bless you for standing with us.

We have now launched the next phase: constructing and equipping part of the facility so we can stop renting and begin hosting Christian Restoration Network programs on-site by October 2026.

The budget for this phase is **30 million FCFA ($53,000)**, covering construction and essential equipment. This space will host prayer, discipleship, leadership training, and counseling.

We invite you to partner with us. **300 partners giving 100,000 FCFA ($165)** each will meet this need, though every gift counts.

To Partner with us, send your gifts to :

652 382 693
(Ketu Isaac Nembo)

696 565 864
(Ketu Isaac Nembo)

0040812604565101
(Tangumonkem Godson Nembo)

godsonnembo@gmail.com

For inquiries contact:
677 436 964 / 673 540 233

Together, we can raise an altar that will bless generations.
Thank you, and may God richly bless you.

CHRISTIAN RESTORATION NETWORK
The RESTORATION House
Pastors Godson & Anna Tangumonkem
Current progress of the project
1
2
Progress of works
3
Laying of the foundation stone
4
For inquiries contact:
677 436 964 / 673 540 233
Together, we can raise an altar that will bless generations.
Thank you, and may God richly bless you.

PRAYER STORM

DAILY PRAYER GUIDE

RECOVER ALL

MAY – JUNE 2026

Godson T. Nembo

RECOVER ALL

Published in Cameroon by:
Christian Restoration Network
crnprayerstorm@gmail.com,
prayerstorm@christianrestorationnetwork.org

ISBN: 978-1-63603-347-1

All scripture quotations are from the New King James Version (NKJV) of the Bible except otherwise stated.

CONTACT

P.O. Box 31339 Biyem-assi, Yaounde, Cameroon
Tel.: 679.46.57.17, 652.38.26.93 or 696.56.58.64
Email: **godsonnembo@gmail.com** or
contact@christianrestorationnetwork.org
www.christianrestorationnetwork.org
www.christianrestorationnetwork.org

WHERE TO BUY THIS PRAYER GUIDE:
SEE THE LAST PAGE

YOU CAN ACCESS ALL PRINTED HARD COPIES OF OUR BOOKS FOR ANY SPECIFIED DURATION AT YOUR DOORSTEP.

Contact (237) 679465717 for subscription and payment details.

Prayer Storm Online Store: With MTN or Orange Mobile Money *(for those in Cameroon)* and E-Wallet *(for those abroad)*, you can easily obtain the electronic version of this book and other CRN publications via **www.amazon.com** at **https://shorturl.at/pqxyT** or **www.christianrestorationnetwork.org/our-bookstore** or **https://goo.gl/ktf3rT**

Printed in Yaounde, Cameroon by Mama press: (237) 677581523

TESTIMONIES:

Your testimony is a weapon against the kingdom of darkness. It is also a seed for someone else's miracle. Share with us what God has used this prayer guide and our books to do in your life; by SMS, telephone call or email.

BECOME A MINISTRY PARTNER:

Call the numbers: (237) 679.46.57.17 or 652.38.26.93 or 696.56.58.64 or send an email to:

crnprayerstorm@gmail.com or

contact@christianrestorationnetwork.org

Send your financial seed to:

- ECOBANK Acc. N°: **0040812604565101**
- Carmel Cooperative Credit Union Ltd. Bamenda Acc. N°: **261**
- ORANGE Mobile Money Acc. N°: **699902618**
- MTN Mobile Money Acc. N°: **674495895**

A NEED FOR DISTRIBUTORS:

If you are interested in the distribution of this Prayer Storm Daily Prayer Guide, call or send an SMS to any of these numbers for negotiations: (237) 675.68.60.05 or 677.43.69.64 or 652.38.26.93 or 696.56.58.64 or send an email to: **crnprayerstorm@gmail.com** (see last page).

TABLE OF CONTENTS

IMPORTANT EVENTS/ANNOUNCEMENTS

SPECIAL PRAYER PROGRAM			
RESTORATION PRAYER CAMP 10th Edition	**Venue**	**Theme**	**From Thursday 6th to Saturday 8th August 2026**
	Yaounde, Cameroon Prepare to take part	***WHEN GOD VISITS A FAMILY***	

Register immediately online via
https://forms.gle/KfUyegrM5EeJXgP38.
Participation is FREE but lodging is payable, Make your reservations as soon as possible.
WhatsApp Contact: (237) 681722404 or 679465717 or Call: (237) 695722340 or 652382693.

SPECIAL PRAYER STORM PROGRAM			
5 NIGHTS OF POWER WITH PASTOR GODSON	**Theme**	**Date**	**Join us daily at midnight (GMT +1) on YouTube, Facebook**
	RECOVER ALL	*From Friday 1st to Tuesday 5th May 2026*	

SPECIAL PROGRAM: I PRAY FOR YOU
Join Pastor Godson for a half hour morning devotion every **MONDAY, WEDNESDAY, and FRIDAY** from **6am** live on Facebook, YouTube **@PastorGodsonNemboTangumonkem**

HOUR OF RESTORATION

Join Pastor Godson & Anna TANGUMONKEM for HOUR OF RESTORATION **every TUESDAY** morning from **6 – 7:30am** in the banquet hall: Salle des fêtes « Fontaine de grâce » at Jouvence, Mendong street – Yaounde, Cameroon..

A time of prophetic intercession for individuals, families and the nations.

ANNOUNCEMENTS

- Festival of Fire series No. 1-5 and Power Must Change Hands Vol. 1-10 now available at XAF 3,000. Send your orders from today.
- Annual subscription to the Daily Prayer Guide from XAF 10,000 for electronic copies.
- All our books are available at our CRN Head office: 1st Floor Storey Building at Entrée Lycée de Tsinga village on the edge of the main road. **Contact:** 681.72.24.04, 695.72.23.40
- Carmel Credit Union, Yaoundé branch located at Carrefour Biyem-Assi, on the ground floor of the storey building, opposite Campus Crusade for Christ. **Contact:** +237 652.83.55.04
- Prayer Storm Bookshop at Cow Street Nkwen – Bamenda sells our books, Bibles and excellent Christian literature. **Contact:** 675.14.04.50, 674.59.35.98, 679.46.57.17.

"RESTORATION CAMP" Project

- The project for the establishment of the base for CRN in Yaounde, Cameroon began in January 2020.

- The LAYING OF THE FOUNDATION STONE FOR THE RESTORATION PRAYER HOUSE at Tsinga Village, Yaounde, took place in December 2023.
- For information on how to be part of the project, call or send SMS to **(237) 674.49.58.95, 678.16.46.88, 673.50.42.33, 699.90.26.18.**

Feedback Questionnaire:

We will love to hear your suggestions on how we can improve on this book: Send your comments to **(237) 681722404**, use the link https://prayer-stormdevotional.paperform.com/ or scan the QR CODE shown here to fill the online form.

HOW TO BECOME A CHILD OF GOD

Going to church and praying is not enough. *"Except a man is BORN AGAIN, he CANNOT SEE the kingdom of God." (John 3:3).*

The following steps will help you know how you can be born again.

Step 1: God Loves You and Offers a Wonderful Plan for Your Life

"For God so loved the world that He gave His only begotten Son, that whoever believes in Him should not perish but have everlasting life" (John 3:16). Jesus said, "*I came that they might have life and have it to the full." (John 10:10).*

No matter who you are and what you have done, God still loves you and wants to save you (Rom.5:8).

Step 2: Your Sins Have Separated You from God; That Is Why You Are Not Experiencing His Wonderful Plan for Your Life

"For all have sinned and fall short of the glory of God" (Rom.3:23)

"The wages of sin is death (spiritual separation from God) Rom.6:23.

All your religious activities and efforts cannot save you. God has provided a solution for you.

Step 3: Jesus Christ Is the Only Way Back to God

Jesus said, *"I am the way, the truth and the life, No one comes to the father except through me" (John 14:6).* Jesus is the only sacrifice God can accept for your sins. Through Him you can connect to God's plan for your life.

Step 4: You Must Personally Receive Jesus Christ as Your Saviour and Lord. Then You Can Know and Experience God's Plan for Your Life

Receive Him by personal invitation and by faith. *"Behold, I stand at the door and knock. If anyone hears My voice and opens the door (your heart), I will come in to him and dine with him, and he with Me." (Rev.3:20).*

If you are ready now to give your life to Jesus Christ, pray this prayer with all your heart.

"Dear Lord Jesus Christ, I need you. I open the door of my life and receive you as my Saviour and Lord. Forgive all my sins and wash me with your blood. Make me the kind of person you want me to be. Thank you for saving me."

Congrats! You are now a child of God.

Call us now let us pray for you: (237) 652.38.26.93 or 696.56.58.64

(Pastor Godson T. Nembo & Prayer Storm Team)

NOW THAT YOU ARE BORN AGAIN

Making the decision to become a born-again Christian, is the best decision you've ever made in your entire life and I congratulate you for that. The following points will help you enjoy your newfound life in Christ Jesus.

1. **Live with the Consciousness that You are Saved:** It is fundamental that you are certain of your new faith. This is referred to as the Assurance of Salvation. Believe that your sins have been forgiven and forgotten by God because of the price Jesus paid by His sacrificial death on the cross and that you are no longer under any condemnation (Acts 16:31, Rom.8:1-2, 2Cor.5:17, Jn.1:12).

2. **Join a Fellowship:** By new birth, you have entered the family of God. Locate a church that teaches and practises the scriptures truthfully, where the worship enables you to encounter God, and where the people are friendly and spiritual growth is encouraged (Heb.10:25, Gal.6:10).

3. **Get a Bible and Study It Daily:** You can begin from John, then Acts, Romans, etc. Just as a baby needs physical nourishment in order to grow, the Word of God is also the spiritual food by which we grow into Christlikeness (1Pet.2:2, Jn.5:24). Consult other mature Christians for any explanations.

4. **Commune Daily with God:** Through prayer, we talk with God, express our burdens to Him, as well as offer worship, praise and appreciation. We also have the privilege to get God speak to us, showering upon us His

love, peace, blessings and divine direction (Rom.10:9, 1Thess.5:17, 1Pet.5:8).

5. **Destroy Satan's Property in Your Keeping:** Desist from anything that does not glorify God. Do away with anything evil related to your sinful past, such as pornographic materials, stolen money and possessions, talismans, charms, juju, etc. (2Cor.6:17, Tit.2:11).

6. **Separate from Evil Friends and Get New Godly Friends:** Now that you are born again, you must discontinue the former way of life and walk in the truth (Ps.1:1-3, 2Cor.4:2; 5:17, Eph.4:22, 1Jn.1:6).

7. **Get Baptized:** Water baptism by immersion publicly authenticates our salvation and affirms our membership in the body of Christ (Rom.6:4, Col.2:12, Matt.28:19, Acts 2:38, 8:36).

8. **Seek the Baptism of the Holy Spirit:** The Holy Spirit assures us that we are saved and empowers us to live a holy life and do exploits for God through special gifts (Rom.8:14, Acts 2:1-4; 10:38, Eph.5:18).

9. **Tell Others about Jesus:** Our character should testify about our inner transformation. Also, our eagerness to tell others about God's love and lead them to Christ is also evidential about our salvation (Jn.4:28-29, Acts 4:10; 22:14, 2Tim.2:2).

10. **Worship God with Your Wealth through Offerings and Tithes:** Our cheerful giving is essential in advancing God's Kingdom – freewill offerings and tithe (one-tenth of our increase) (Deut.16:16-17, Prov.3:9-10, 2Cor:9:7).

11. **Make the Life of Christ Your Standard:** Fix your eyes on Jesus, the Author and Finisher of our faith Make Him your Role Model (Heb.12:2, Phil.2:5-11, Eph.4:24).

12. **Don't Abandon; Rise and Continue, if you Fall:** The Christian race may seem tough and challenging, with persecutions, distractions, oppositions, and even discouragements. But rest assured, you will make it by faith (Prov.24:16, Isa.41:10, Phil.1:6).

I pray that you will stand firm, and finish well like other heroes of faith, in Jesus' name! Amen.

Call us for counselling and prayer: (237) 652.38.26.93 or 696.56.58.64.

(Pastor Godson T. Nembo & Prayer Storm Team)

HOW TO USE THIS DAILY PRAYER GUIDE

I have discovered that some people do not know how to use this book well. As a result, they are not benefiting much from it. I will like to explain to you, how you can either use it during your personal prayer time or how to use it to lead a group prayer session.

Your Personal Prayer Time:

1. ***Read the topic of the day:*** It is the summary of the message of the day.
2. ***Read the Bible passages of the day aloud:*** You retain more, when you read aloud to yourself. In the early days, scriptures were read aloud.
3. ***Read the meditation slowly:*** Do it with a strong desire to understand.
4. ***Pray the prayer points:*** Read each prayer point and take time to pray well before you read the next one.
5. ***Pray for others:*** Use the prayer point to pray for other people as inspired by the Holy Spirit.
6. ***Add other prayer topics:*** For instance; dedicate your day, your family, your job, your Church, etc. to God.
7. Pray for your specific needs and those of others.
8. ***Action/Declaration:*** Take practical steps and do the prophetic declarations.
9. ***Prophetic Prayers of the Week:*** These prayers will be brought up every Monday. We encourage you to pray them every day during the week that follows.

Leading a Group to Pray:

1. Read the topic of the day aloud.
2. Assign one or more persons to read the Bible passage of the day aloud.

3. Read the meditation of the day aloud. After reading, you can make some comments, if necessary.
4. Allow other members of the group to make contributions or ask questions, if they have them.
5. Read one prayer point at a time. Then allow the people to pray for some time before you read the next one.
6. After they have prayed in chorus, you can ask one person to raise his/her voice and pray.
7. When you finish reading the prayer points, first ask the group members to give their own personal prayer plan.
8. At the end, let one person pray and conclude the session.

Bible Reading Plan:

We have included two Bible reading plans: **"Bible in 1 year"** and **"Bible in 2 years."** You can read through your Bible in one year by following the first plan in two years by following the second plan. Set aside time every day to read your Bible.

Friday 1 May

RECOVERING ALL THROUGH THE CROSS

Read: Colossians 2:13-15;
John 19:30

Bible in 1 year: Luke 22-24
Bible in 2 years: Num. 19-20

"Having disarmed principalities and powers, He made a public spectacle of them, triumphing over them in it" (Colossians 2:15).

Every recovery we are talking about this month – spiritual fire, prayer altar, calling, joy, finances, relationships, dominion – finds its foundation at the Cross. Without the Cross, there is no true recovery. With the Cross, nothing is permanently lost.

When Jesus cried, *"It is finished,"* He was not expressing defeat; He was declaring completion. The debt of sin was canceled. Shame was broken. Authority was restored. Access to the Father was reopened. The enemy was disarmed forever. And the gateway to the blessing was opened to those who come to Christ.

In the Garden of Eden, humanity lost dominion, intimacy, and righteousness. But at Calvary, Christ – the second Adam recovered what the first Adam forfeited. What was lost through Adam's disobedience was restored through Christ's obedience (Romans 5:19).

Think about Job. After a disastrous loss, Scripture says the Lord restored his fortunes and gave him twice as much as he had before (Job 42:10). Job's story foreshadows the greater restoration secured for us in Christ. The Cross is

God's ultimate declaration that loss does not have the final word. With God, nothing is lost!

Sometimes we attempt recovery through effort alone – through self-improvement, strategy, and discipline. These are valuable, but incomplete without total surrender to Jesus Christ. True enlargement flows from redemption. Some people naively say, "Stop praying and go to work." No! The right thing to say is, "While praying, go to work."

The Cross does not merely restore you to your previous state; it elevates you. You are not just forgiven; you are adopted into God's family. Not just cleansed; you are commissioned to impact your generation. Not just rescued; you are empowered by the indwelling presence of the Holy Spirit to live for God and do exploits (Galatians 4:6).

As you meditate with this book, remember: recovery is not rooted in human determination but in Christ's finished work. Stand on what He has accomplished for you on the cross. Through the Cross, you recover all. Walk in this truth daily by faith, in Jesus' name.

Action: *Today, spend time meditating on the finished work of Christ and thank God for specific areas of restoration in your life.*

Let us pray

1. *Father, thank You for the finished work of Christ on the Cross, in Jesus' name.*
2. *Lord, help me depend fully on Your grace for restoration, in Jesus' name.*
3. *Holy Spirit, teach me to walk in the victory Christ secured for me on the cross, in Jesus' name.*
4. *Father, let the reign of the risen Christ be established in every area of my life, in Jesus' name*

5. *As I travel through this month, let the power of divine restoration dominate every area of my life and ministry, in Jesus' name.*

Saturday 2 May **CHECK YOUR FOUNDATION**

Read: 2 Timothy 2:19-21

Bible in 1 year: Judg. 1-4
Bible in 2 years: Num. 21; 22:1-20

"Nevertheless, the solid foundation of God stands, having this seal: 'The Lord knows those who are His,' and, 'Let everyone who names the name of Christ depart from iniquity'" (2 Timothy 2:19).

In architecture, the depth of the foundation determines the height of a storey building. The same principle applies to our spiritual enlargement. Maybe your primary concern is to attain the "height" of power, influence, and prosperity, but God is primarily concerned with the "depth" of your holiness. Holiness is not a decorative ornament on your Christian life; it is the structural foundation that allows you to carry the weight of God's glory without cracking.

Our scripture today tells us that in a "great house," there are various vessels. Some are for honor and some for dishonor. The difference isn't determined by the material we are made of, but by our level of consecration. If you cleanse yourself from the "dishonorable" things (the secret sins, the compromised integrity, and the double-mindedness), you become a vessel of gold, "sanctified and useful for the Master." God is looking for utility, and in His house, utility is always preceded by purity.

Set a guard over your heart. It is the realization that being "set apart" is not a burden, but a promotion. When you choose to depart from iniquity, you aren't missing out on life; you are qualifying for a higher level of operation.

Today, ask yourself: Is my foundation deep enough to support the blessings I am asking God for? Enlargement without holiness is a recipe for a tragic fall, but a holy foundation ensures a lasting legacy.

Action: *Spend 10 minutes today in "foundation check." Ask the Holy Spirit to point out one area of compromise you have ignored, and repent of it immediately.*

Let us pray

1. *Father, I thank You for the grace to be called by Your name.*
2. *Lord, search my heart and expose every crack in my spiritual foundation.*
3. *O Lord, grant me the strength to depart from every form of iniquity today.*
4. *Father, purge me and make me a vessel of honor, fit for Your use.*
5. *Holy Spirit, help me to value my consecration above my comfort.*

Sunday 3 May

WARFARE AGAINST FOUNDATIONAL STRONGHOLDS

Read: Judges 6:25-26;
2 Corinthians 10:3-5

Bible in 1 year: Judg. 5-8
Bible in 2 years: Num. 22:21-41; 23

"For the weapons of our warfare are not carnal but mighty in God for pulling down strongholds" (2 Corinthians 10:4).

Total recovery begins at the foundation. Many believers pray for enlargement while standing on damaged foundations. Foundational strongholds are deeply rooted patterns, mindsets, or spiritual altars that shape beliefs, behavior, and outcomes. These foundations are sometimes inherited or cultivated over time.

In Judges 6, before Gideon could deliver Israel from Midian, God instructed him to tear down his father's altar to Baal and build a new altar to the Lord. National oppression was linked to a foundational compromise. Deliverance began at home.

Strongholds may not always be demonic altars; they can be destructive beliefs – "Nothing good lasts in my family," "We never succeed," "We are poor, and there is nothing we can do to change it," "Failure is normal," "Our destinies are locked up in a pot." Such thoughts quietly govern decisions. Paul tells us that warfare involves pulling down arguments and every high thing that exalts itself against the knowledge of God.

At the Cross, Jesus became our true foundation. He is the Chief Cornerstone (Ephesians 2:20). When Christ becomes the basis of identity and thinking, old structures collapse. The enemy builds through deception; Christ restores through truth.

Consider a building with cracked pillars. Renovating the walls will not secure it. The foundation must be repaired. Likewise, recovery demands spiritual confrontation. Prayer, repentance, renunciation of wrong beliefs, and declaration of God's Word are tools of warfare.

Enlargement cannot stand on compromised ground. Gideon rebuilt the altar before leading the battle. You must rebuild on Christ before advancing.

When the foundation is corrected, oppression loses legal ground. Christ has already secured victory; warfare enforces it. Total recovery begins with the repair of foundations.

Action: *Identify one destructive pattern or belief in your life and confront it with Scripture this week.*

Let us pray

1. *Father, thank You that Christ is my sure foundation, in Jesus' name.*
2. *Lord, expose and uproot every foundational stronghold in my life, in Jesus' name.*
3. *Holy Spirit, renew my mind with truth that liberates, in Jesus' name.*
4. *Father, break every inherited negative pattern affecting my destiny, in Jesus' name*
5. *As I begin to pray right now, let every force of darkness reinforcing strongholds in my life scatter by fire, in Jesus' name.*

Monday 4 May

THE URGENCY OF THE CROSS

Read: Galatians 2:20–21

Bible in 1 year: Judg. 9-12
Bible in 2 years: Num. 24-25

"I have been crucified with Christ and I no longer live, but Christ lives in me." (Galatians 2:20)

Salvation is not merely a ticket to heaven; it is an invitation to a radical exchange of life. Paul describes this as being "crucified with Christ." This imagery is not about mere moral improvement; it is about the total death of the old self—the nature that was governed by ego, pride, and sin. When we embrace the cross, we acknowledge that our old identity is no longer in charge. In its place, the very life of Christ begins to manifest. This is the heart of the Christian walk: the daily surrender of our personal will to His divine direction.

Many believers struggle because they want the benefits of Christ without the surrender of the cross. They try to "add" Jesus to their existing lifestyle rather than allowing Him to replace it. However, Scripture tells us that this exchange is non-negotiable. You cannot hold onto the steering wheel of your life and expect Christ to be the driver. The "crucifixion" of the flesh is a continuous, daily process of saying "no" to our own desires so that we can say "yes" to His leading. It is a death that leads to true, resurrection-powered life.

Are you living a life that is truly "hidden" in Christ, or are you still trying to preserve your old self? The cross is a place of surrender. When we stop trying to maintain our own reputation, security, and agenda, we finally open the door for the Holy Spirit to take full control. Today, make the conscious choice to release your grip on your own life. When you die to yourself, you discover that the life you now live is filled with a power that is not your own.

Prophetic Declaration: *I have been crucified with Christ! My old nature is dead, and the life I now live is empowered by the Spirit of God.*

Let us pray

1. *Father, I surrender my old identity and everything that keeps me from You.*
2. *Father, crucify my pride and selfish ambition so Your life can shine through me.*
3. *Holy Spirit, replace my own desires with the heart and will of Jesus.*
4. *O Lord, teach me how to die to my self-will daily.*
5. *I receive the resurrection power of Christ to live a life that honors Him!*

Prophetic Prayer of the Week

1. ***"David recovered all that the Amalekites had carried away." (1 Samuel 30:18).*** *I am recovering everything the enemy has stolen from my life, in Jesus' name.*
2. ***"I will restore health to you and heal you of your wounds." (Jeremiah 30:17).*** *My body receives total healing and divine health, in Jesus' name.*
3. ***"My peace I give to you." (John 14:27).*** *Every storm in my heart is silenced, and my peace is restored, in Jesus' name.*

Tuesday 5 May **FAITH IN THE BLOOD**

Read: Romans 5:6–11

Bible in 1 year: Judg. 13-15
Bible in 2 years: Num. 26

"Much more then, having now been justified by His blood, we shall be saved from wrath through Him" (Romans 5:9)

The doctrine of the blood of Jesus is not merely a theological concept; it is the absolute foundation of our standing before a holy God. Paul, writing to the Romans, emphasizes that our justification—our legal acquittal in the court of Heaven—is provided exclusively by the blood of Christ. In the ancient covenant, blood was the price of life and the means of atonement. Under the new covenant, Christ's blood is the eternal currency that settled the infinite debt of our sin. When we embrace this truth, we are confronted with the reality that salvation is entirely a work of grace. As Ephesians 2:8–9 reminds us, we are saved by grace through faith, and this is not a result of our own works, so that no man can boast.

Faith in the blood of Jesus acts as a corrective to human pride. When we try to justify ourselves through our talents, our church attendance, or our "good deeds," we essentially claim that Christ's sacrifice was insufficient. True faith humbles us. It recognizes that we were once "far off" but have been brought near by the blood. This faith is not a passive acceptance; it is a profound trust that leans entirely on the efficacy of the cross. Just as the Israelites in Egypt had to apply the blood to their doorposts to be spared from judgment, we must apply the blood of Christ to the doorposts of our hearts, trusting that it is the only shield against the wrath we truly deserve.

Are you resting in the finished work of the cross, or are you still trying to earn your way into God's favor? Many believers live in unnecessary spiritual poverty because they refuse to accept the sufficiency of what Jesus did. Your past failures, your current struggles, and your future shortcomings were all covered at Calvary. Faith in the blood is the ultimate antidote to the enemy's accusations. Whenever you feel unworthy or defeated, return to this truth: you have been justified, not by your own perfection, but by His precious blood.

Action: *Spend dedicated time today meditating on the cross of Christ, specifically thanking Jesus for the blood that saves, cleanses, and justifies you.*

Let us pray

1. *Lord, deepen my faith in the efficacy of Your precious sacrifice at Calvary.*
2. *Help me to trust Your blood alone, not my merit or works, for my salvation.*
3. *Deliver me from the pride of relying on my own human effort to gain Your favor.*
4. *Let Your grace, poured out through the blood, transform my life from the inside out.*
5. *Keep me humble and constantly grateful before the reality of the Cross.*

Wednesday 6 May

RESTORATION OF YOUR SPIRITUAL AUTHORITY

Read: Luke 10:17-20;
Genesis 1:26-28

Bible in 1 year: Judg. 16-18
Bible in 2 years: Num. 27-28

"Behold, I give you authority… OVER ALL THE POWER OF THE ENEMY" (Luke 10:19).

One of the greatest losses in a believer's life is the loss of spiritual confidence. You have been given legal authority in Christ, but maybe you are not using it. Fear, sin, intimidation, or repeated failure may be causing you to shrink back. When you fail to exercise your spiritual authority, dominion is surrendered.

From the beginning, God created humanity to have dominion. Sin distorted that authority, but Christ restored it. In Luke 10, the seventy returned rejoicing that demons were subject to them. Jesus affirmed their authority but redirected their focus to relationship: *"Rejoice because your names are written in heaven."*

Our spiritual authority flows from our union with Christ. It is not personality strength; it is delegated power from the Lord. When Peter walked on water, authority operated as long as his focus remained on Jesus. When fear replaced faith, he began to sink.

Many believers pray timidly because guilt weakens their confidence. Compromise paralyzes their boldness. A soldier cannot fight effectively if he doubts his commission and the weapons he carries. That is why repentance is essential in warfare. Deal with sin before you declare war against Satan. Clean hands restore confidence (Psalm 24:3-4).

Consider a police officer who forgets he carries legal authority. Criminals would dominate unnecessarily. Likewise, believers who forget their identity allow the oppressor to torment them.

At the Cross, Jesus disarmed principalities (Colossians 2:15). The victory is complete. Warfare is not fighting for victory; it is enforcing what Christ accomplished for us.

Enlargement demands dominion. You cannot expand territory while living intimidated. Stand in righteousness. Speak with faith. Act in obedience. Your authority is restored in Christ. Rise and exercise it.

Action: *Declare specific Scriptures boldly over one area where fear is trying to limit you.*

Let us pray

1. *Father, thank You for restoring my authority through Jesus Christ, in Jesus' name.*
2. *Lord, remove from my life anything that weakens my boldness, in Jesus' name.*
3. *Holy Spirit, strengthen my faith with fire to exercise dominion over the powers of darkness, in Jesus' name.*
4. *I silence every voice of intimidation speaking against my destiny, in Jesus' name.*
5. *I speak to the heavens over me; open let the glory of God overshadow me, in Jesus' name.*

Thursday 7 May

YOU ARE GOD'S BATTLE AXE

Read: Jeremiah 51:20–23;
2 Corinthians 10:3–5

Bible in 1 year: Judg.19-21
Bible in 2 years: Num. 29-30

"You are My battle axe and weapons of war: for with you I will break the nation in pieces" (Jeremiah 51:20).

God once spoke to Israel, calling them His battle axe. A battle axe is not ornamental; it is purposeful, sharp, and intentional. It is an instrument in the hand of a warrior. The power is not in the axe itself, but in the one who wields it.

In Christ, believers are God's instruments on earth. We are not spectators in the ongoing spiritual conflict; we are participants. However, an axe lying on the ground is ineffective. It must remain in the hand of the Master.

Many believers either underestimate or misuse their spiritual authority. Some shrink back in fear. Others fight in the flesh. But Scripture reminds us that the weapons of our warfare are not carnal. God's battle axe does not operate through anger, manipulation, or human strength. It operates through prayer, truth, righteousness, and obedience.

Consider David before Goliath. He had no armor, but he was fully yielded to God. In God's hand, a shepherd boy became a weapon of victory. The strength was not in David; it was in the Lord of hosts.

Being God's battle axe means a life of total surrender to Jesus Christ. An axe must be sharpened. Prayer sharpens. Holiness sharpens. Discipline sharpens. Without sharpening, even a strong tool becomes dull.

At the Cross, Jesus disarmed principalities and powers. Now, He works through yielded vessels to enforce that victory. You are not fighting for triumph; you are fighting from triumph.

Enlargement requires spiritual readiness. When God raises you as His instrument, resistance will come, but so will grace.

Remain in His hand. Stay sharp in the Spirit. And allow Him to use you for victory.

Action: *Examine your spiritual sharpness this week and commit to consistent prayer and holiness.*

Let us pray

1. *Father, thank You for choosing me as Your instrument, in Jesus' name.*
2. *Lord, remove fear and insecurity from my heart, in Jesus' name.*
3. *Holy Spirit, sharpen me through prayer and obedience, in Jesus' name.*
4. *Father, keep me yielded and useful in Your hand, in Jesus' name.*
5. *I attack and cut down every Goliath oppressing the destiny of my family, in Jesus' name.*

Friday 8 May **RECOVER YOUR CALLING**

Read: Romans 11:29;
2 Timothy 1:6-9

Bible in 1 year: Ruth 1-4
Bible in 2 years: Num. 31

"For the gifts and the calling of God are irrevocable" (Romans 11:29).

There are moments in life when discouragement, delay, criticism, or failure make you question your calling. You once heard God clearly. You once burned with conviction. But opposition arose, doors closed, and confidence weakened. Slowly, you stepped back. In my early days of the pastoral ministry, I almost abandoned my call because of hardship. Some people even said I was not called.

Your calling is God's divine assignment upon your life. It is not a self-appointed ambition; it is heaven's design. Yet calling can be buried under fear, comparison, or disappointment. Confusion and frustration set in when you abandon your divine calling.

Consider Jeremiah. When persecution intensified, he declared, *"I will not make mention of Him."* Yet he later confessed that God's word was like fire shut up in his bones (Jeremiah 20:9). He could not abandon what heaven had planted within him.

Or think of Peter. After denying Jesus, he returned to fishing – the very occupation he had left to follow the Lord. It was as though he were retreating from his apostolic calling. But in John 21, the risen Christ met him, restored him, and recommissioned him: *"Feed My sheep."* Seasonal failure did not cancel his assignment.

Maybe you want to abandon your calling because results are slow. Maybe you feel inadequate because you are comparing yourself to others. Or you may have been wounded deeply by criticism. But Scripture says God's calling is irrevocable. If He called you, He has not changed His mind.

Recovering your calling begins by returning to Christ, not chasing platforms. Paul told Timothy to *"stir up the gift of God."* Gifts must be rekindled intentionally. Prayer, obedience, study, and faithfulness fan the flame again.

Enlargement comes when you embrace your divine assignment with renewed courage. What discouragement tried to silence, Christ can restore. Your calling is not lost; it is simply waiting for you to rise again.

Action: *Write down your God-given calling and take one practical step this week to re-engage it.*

Let us pray

1. *Father, thank You for calling me according to Your purpose, in Jesus' name.*
2. *Lord, forgive me for doubting or shrinking back from my assignment, in Jesus' name.*
3. *Holy Spirit, rekindle every dormant gift within me today, in Jesus' name.*
4. *Father, heal every wound caused by criticism or disappointment, in Jesus' name.*
5. *I decree that I am rising boldly into my calling and I am recovering all, in Jesus' name*

Saturday 9 May

RECOVERING LOST VISION

Read: Proverbs 29:18;
Habakkuk 2:1-3

Bible in 1 year: 1Pet. 1-2
Bible in 2 years: Num. 32

"Where there is no vision, the people perish" (Proverbs 29:18).

Vision is the ability to see tomorrow through the lens of God's promises. When vision is lost, direction is lost. When direction is lost, energy is wasted. Many believers are not defeated by the enemy; they are defeated by blurred vision. God wants to restore your ability to see clearly for speed this year.

There was a time when you saw clearly what God wanted to do through your life, your family, or your ministry. You wrote plans. You prayed with excitement. But delay, hardship, or opposition has clouded your sight. Gradually, survival has come to replace your purpose. You now run without conviction. You are no longer sure of what God is doing in your life.

Consider Abraham. God showed him the stars and promised descendants beyond number. Yet years passed without a child. At one point, Abraham suggested Eliezer as his heir (Genesis 15:2-3). Delay tested his vision. But God brought him outside again and reaffirmed the promise. Vision had to be renewed.

Or think of the disciples on the road to Emmaus (Luke 24:13-32). After the crucifixion, their vision collapsed They said, *"We were hoping…" (v. 21).* Hope had shifted to disappointment. But when Jesus opened the Scriptures, their hearts burned again. Vision returned when Christ was revealed to them afresh.

Vision fades when prayer weakens. It fades when comparison distracts. It fades when we focus more on obstacles than on God's word. But vision can be recovered. Habakkuk climbed the watchtower to wait for God's voice. Renewal begins when we position ourselves to hear from God again.

Enlargement requires clear sight. You cannot expand what you cannot see. Ask God to restore clarity in your life. Let Christ redefine your perspective. The One who gave the promise is faithful to fulfill it.

Lost vision is not final; it is recoverable in the presence of God.

Action: *Take a time of retreat. Revisit God's promises concerning you. Rewrite your vision.*

Let us pray

1. *Father, thank You for the vision You have spoken over my life, in Jesus' name.*
2. *Lord, forgive me for allowing discouragement to blur my spiritual sight, in Jesus' name.*
3. *Holy Spirit, restore clarity and direction to my destiny this season, in Jesus' name.*
4. *Father, renew my hope where delay has weakened my faith, in Jesus' name.*
5. *I receive fresh fire for the restoration of my vision for divine enlargement, in Jesus' name.*

Sunday 10 May **THE AMBASSADOR'S AUTHORITY**

Read: 2 Corinthians 5:20–21

Bible in 1 year: 1Pet. 3-6
Bible in 2 years: Num. 33

"We are therefore Christ's ambassadors, as though God were making His appeal through us." (2 Corinthians 5:20)

An ambassador does not speak on their own authority; they speak on behalf of the government they represent. When we recognize that we are "Christ's ambassadors," our perspective on daily interactions changes. We are not just navigating our own careers, families, or social circles; we are carrying the weight and the message of the Kingdom of Heaven into those spaces. The authority we carry as ambassadors is not derived from our charisma or our status, but from the One who commissioned us.

Many believers feel powerless in their environments because they forget their official standing. They try to convince others through argument or human persuasion, forgetting that the ambassador's true power lies in the message of the King. When you represent Christ, you are not trying to win an argument; you are offering an invitation to reconciliation. This requires us to live in a way that aligns with the character of the King we represent. If our lives do not reflect the peace, holiness, and love of Christ, our message loses its credibility.

If people only knew what they saw in your daily life, what would they conclude about the King you serve?

Ambassadors must be both clear in their message and consistent in their conduct. Today, walk with the confidence of an ambassador. Know that you have been sent into your specific sphere of influence with the mandate of Heaven. When you speak, speak as one who carries the King's authority.

Prophetic Declaration: *I am an ambassador for the King of Kings! My life represents His truth, my words carry His authority, and I am effective in my ministry of reconciliation!*

Let us pray

1. *Father, thank You for the honor of representing You as an ambassador in this world.*
2. *Lord, align my character with the message I carry so that my life reflects Your truth.*
3. *Holy Spirit, grant me the boldness to speak for You in every situation I face today.*
4. *O Lord, let my presence in my workplace and home be a clear witness of Your reconciling love.*
5. *I receive the grace to operate with the authority of the King in all my interactions!*

Monday 11 May

RECOVERING FROM PRAYERLESSNESS

Read: Luke 22:39-46

Bible in 1 year: 2Pet. 1-3
Bible in 2 years: Num. 34-35

"Watch and pray, lest you enter into temptation" (Luke 22:46).

What will you say about yourself? Are you prayerful or prayerless?

Prayerlessness is never harmless. When we neglect prayer, we do not remain neutral; we become vulnerable. Jesus warned His disciples in Gethsemane to watch and pray, to escape the coming temptation. Instead, they slept while He prayed. A moment later, Peter, who was sleeping, pulled out a sword and cut someone's ear. Sadly, he who once boldly declared his loyalty to Christ denied Him three times. What sleep stole, tears later exposed.

Prayerlessness steals sensitivity. It steals discernment. It steals spiritual strength. Samson is another example. He played casually with compromise until *"he did not know that the LORD had departed from him" (Judges 16:20).* His physical strength remained for a moment, but spiritual authority was gone.

When we stop praying, we slowly rely on our own wisdom. We respond emotionally instead of spiritually. We speak before listening to God. Over time, dryness replaces joy, and striving replaces grace.

Consider a soldier who ignores communication from headquarters. He may be brave, but without instructions, he is exposed. Prayer is our lifeline to heaven's strategy. Without it, we fight battles blindly.

But here is hope: what prayerlessness stole can be recovered. After Peter's failure, Jesus restored him. In Acts 2, the same Peter who denied Christ stood boldly and preached with power. What changed? He returned to the place of prayer (Acts 1:14).

Through Christ, we are not condemned; we are invited back. The Cross restored access to the Father. When we rebuild our prayer life, clarity returns. Strength returns. Authority returns.

Enlargement requires communion. If you want to recover lost boldness, peace, and spiritual edge, return to the altar consistently. Prayerlessness may have weakened you, but prayer will restore you.

Action: *Begin with 30 intentional minutes of focused prayer daily and gradually increase your time.*

Let us pray

1. *Father, thank You for restoring me when I drift, in Jesus' name.*
2. *Lord, forgive me for seasons of prayerlessness, in Jesus' name.*
3. *Holy Spirit, awaken hunger for consistent communion with Jesus in my heart, in Jesus' name.*
4. *Father, restore the strength and discernment I lost through neglecting the prayer altar, in Jesus' name.*
5. *I decree that my prayer life is revived and I recover all that was stolen, in Jesus' name.*

Prophetic Prayer of the Week

1. ***"The joy of the Lord is your strength." (Nehemiah 8:10).*** *My joy is restored, and every heaviness leaves my life, in Jesus' name.*
2. ***"The Lord shall supply all your need according to His riches in glory." (Philippians 4:19).*** *My finances are restored, and divine provision flows into my life, in Jesus' name.*
3. ***"I will restore to you the years that the locust has eaten." (Joel 2:25).*** *Every year of loss in my life is redeemed and restored, in Jesus' name.*

Tuesday 12 May

TAKE YOUR PRAYER TO A HIGHER LEVEL

Read: 1 Samuel 1:10–18

Bible in 1 year: 1Thess. 4-5
Bible in 2 years: Num. 36; Deut. 1:1-22

"She was in bitterness of soul, and prayed to the Lord and wept in anguish" (1 Samuel 1:10).

Casual prayers often produce shallow results. Whispered, distracted, hurried prayers rarely move stubborn mountains. When something serious stands before you – a delay, a closed door, a long-standing burden, or a stubborn health issue, God may be saying, *"Change the gear. Go deeper."*
Hannah shows us how.

For years, she prayed for a child, yet nothing changed. Many people would have given up, blaming God or accepting defeat. But Hannah did something different. This time, her prayer shifted levels. She prayed with intensity, focus, and urgency. She poured out her soul before the Lord (v.15). She wept. She refused distractions. She even added a vow of total surrender (v. 11). Her prayer was no longer routine; it became a desperate faith.

That is the difference between saying prayers and travailing in prayer. When Eli first saw her, he thought she was drunk. Why? Because deep prayer can look unusual to casual observers. But heaven recognized her cry. Before she left the temple, peace filled her heart (v. 18). Soon after, Samuel was conceived. Her breakthrough followed her breakthrough in prayer.

So, how do you move your prayer to a higher level? Pray honestly, not religiously. Remove distractions. Persist even when answers delay. Add sacrifice and surrender. Refuse to quit. *"Men always ought to pray and not lose heart"* (Luke 18:1).

Have you given up? Start again. Go deeper. God still answers earnest prayer.

Mountains don't move with sleepy prayers. They move with fiery, faith-filled ones.

Action: *Set aside one focused hour, three times this week, for distraction-free, heartfelt prayer about your biggest burden.*

Let us pray

1. *Father, thank You for hearing and answering my prayers always, in Jesus' name.*
2. *Lord, ignite fresh fire and passion in my prayer life, to pray with power, in Jesus' name.*
3. *Holy Spirit, help me pray with focus and persistence, in Jesus' name.*
4. *Father, remove every discouragement that makes me give up, in Jesus' name.*
5. *Lord, as I cry to You today, turn my long-standing requests into testimonies, in Jesus' name.*

Wednesday 13 May **THE POWER OF PRAYER STORM**

Read: Acts 12:5–17

Bible in 1 year: Psa. 1-3

Bible in 2 years: Deut. 1:23-46; 2

"So Peter was kept in prison, but the church was earnestly praying to God for him." (Acts 12:5)

The "Prayer Storm" is not just a metaphor; it is a biblical reality where collective, focused, and persistent prayer releases the power of God to break chains. In Acts 12, Peter was facing almost certain death, bound by chains and guarded by soldiers. Yet, the believers did not panic or resort to human schemes. They engaged in an "earnest" prayer storm. The Greek word for "earnestly" (*ektenos*) implies stretching out or straining—a level of intensity that mirrors the physical exertion of a runner. This is the kind of prayer that pierces the heavens.

Many situations in our lives remain stagnant because we treat prayer as a ritual rather than a storm. We pray in whispers when we need to cry out in faith. The church's prayer storm in this passage was so potent that it didn't just open a door; it completely bypassed the locks and chains of the prison. This reveals that when we coordinate our prayers with the will of God, there is no barrier that can remain standing. The obstacles you face today—whether they are spiritual, emotional, or practical—are no match for a church that knows how to pray with intensity.

Are you facing a "prison" in your life that seems impenetrable? Do not let the silence of the situation intimidate you into stopping your prayers. Keep the storm of intercession going. Faith is shown in the persistence of our prayer, especially when we don't see immediate results. Today, increase the frequency and intensity of your prayers. When the people of God decide to pray with one accord, Heaven responds.

Prophetic Declaration: *I refuse to be held captive! My prayers are a storm that breaks every chain! I declare that my breakthrough is coming as I continue to pray!*

Let us Pray

1. *Father, ignite a "prayer storm" within my heart that will not stop until I see my breakthrough.*
2. *Lord, break every chain of limitation that the enemy has placed around my life and family.*
3. *O Lord, I align my prayers with Your will today, believing for the impossible to happen.*
4. *Holy Spirit, teach me how to pray with the intensity that moves the hand of God.*
5. *I receive the victory that comes through persistent, earnest, and unified prayer!*

Thursday 14 May **KEEP YOUR MOUTH SHUT**

Read: Luke 23:8–15

Bible in 1 year: Psa. 4-6
Bible in 2 years: Deut. 3; 4:1-24

"The Lord will fight for you; you need only to keep your mouths shut" (Exodus 14:14 MSG).

There are battles God wants to fight on your behalf—battles of false accusation, hatred, character assassination, and hidden plots. But for God to fight, you must learn the discipline of silence. Many people lose victories because they talk too much, react too fast, or explain too loudly. Human nature pushes us to defend ourselves when wronged, insulted, or misrepresented. Yet speaking out of anger or fear often destroys God's strategy. Some blessings have been delayed simply because the mouth moved before the Spirit spoke.

Jesus is our perfect example. When the woman caught in adultery was dragged before Him, He used silence to defuse anger and melt the accusers' hearts. His quietness gave room for divine wisdom. During His trial in Luke 23:8–15, Jesus refused to defend Himself. He knew that silence is not weakness—it is spiritual authority. Isaiah prophesied that although His words are sharp like a sword (Isaiah 49:2), He would not shout or raise His voice in public (Isaiah 42:2). Meekness is not the absence of power; it is the control of power.

1. **When should you keep quiet?** When emotions are high, when you are angry, when someone tries to provoke you, when you lack full information, and

when speaking will not change the situation. Medical studies show that silence reduces stress chemicals and helps the brain think clearly. Silence is often the safest response in conflict.

2. **When should you speak?** Speak when the Holy Spirit gives you peace. Speak to edify, not to attack. Speak to defend the weak, to declare God's Word, and to confess your faith boldly. Jesus spoke only when it aligned with His Father's purpose.

When you master silence, God will speak for you, defend you, and lift you.

Action: *Exercise silence as a weapon to diffuse anger and hear God's voice.*

Let us pray

1. *Father, thank You for being my Defender and my Voice, in Jesus' name.*
2. *Lord, deliver me from every tendency to react with anger or unnecessary speech, in Jesus' name.*
3. *Father, give me the grace to stay silent when silence is Your strategy, in Jesus' name.*
4. *Holy Spirit, teach my tongue to speak only words that bring life, healing, and peace, in Jesus' name.*
5. *I declare that God will fight my battles and my silence will open doors of victory, in Jesus' name.*

Friday 15 May

HOW TO PUNCTURE YOUR ANGER

Read: Ephesians 4:26–32

Bible in 1 year: Psa. 7-9

Bible in 2 years: Deut. 4:25-49; 5

"Better a patient person than a warrior, one with self-control than one who takes a city" (Proverbs 16:32).

Uncontrolled anger is worse than a nuclear bomb. A bomb destroys a place once, but uncontrolled anger can keep exploding again and again—shattering a person's life, wounding a family, dividing a community, and destabilizing a nation. Visit any prison, and you will meet people who did not plan to become criminals. A moment of anger led them to act without thinking, and that single decision redirected their destiny.

Anger itself is not a sin. God designed anger to help us respond to injustice, resist evil, and defend what is right. But when anger stays too long in the heart or becomes uncontrolled, it becomes a poisonous fire. The Bible warns, *"Anger resides in the lap of fools"* (Ecclesiastes 7:9). Medical studies show that chronic anger increases the risk of heart attacks, hypertension, ulcers, and weakened immunity. Spiritually, anger opens doors to the devil (Ephesians 4:27). Emotionally, it blinds judgment. Relationally, it destroys trust and makes wounds harder to heal.

To puncture anger,

1. **Pause before you act**: Proverbs 14:29 says, *"Whoever is patient has great understanding."* A simple rule like counting one to ten, drinking water, or stepping away helps the brain move from reaction to reasoning.

2. **Pray immediately**: When Nehemiah heard troubling news, he prayed before responding (Nehemiah 2:4). Prayer cools the heart and invites the Holy Spirit to guide our emotions.
3. **Speak slowly and softly**: Science confirms that lowering your voice calms the brain and reduces emotional intensity. Proverbs 15:1 teaches, *"A gentle answer turns away wrath."*
4. **Forgive quickly**: Holding offense fuels anger. Jesus calls us to forgive so we can heal.
5. **Reflect on consequences**: Many testimonies from reformed prisoners show that thinking about future consequences would have stopped their fatal actions.

Ask God to give you a calm spirit that defeats anger before it defeats you.

Action: *Decide to apply the rules above anytime you get angry this week.*

Let us pray

1. *Father, thank You for giving me emotions and the grace to control them, in Jesus' name.*
2. *Father, deliver me from every form of uncontrolled anger that seeks to destroy my destiny, in Jesus' name.*
3. *Lord, fill my heart with the Holy Spirit so that patience and wisdom will lead my reactions, in Jesus' name.*
4. *Father, heal every wound and memory that fuels anger within me, in Jesus' name.*
5. *I declare that anger will not rule my life; I walk in peace, wisdom, and self-control from today, in Jesus' name.*

Saturday 16 May

4 RULES TO INTERPRET YOUR DREAMS

Read: Job 33:14–16;
Daniel 2:19–22

Bible in 1 year: Psa. 10-12
Bible in 2 years: Deut. 6-7

"Do not interpretations belong to God?" (Genesis 40:8).

God can speak through dreams, but not every dream carries divine meaning. Scripture shows that interpretation belongs to God, not human imagination. Joseph and Daniel both depended on God for dream interpretation. If your dreams are mishandled, they can lead to fear, confusion, or poor decisions.

Here are four biblical rules for interpreting dreams:

1. ***Submit Every Dream to Scripture:*** God never contradicts His Word. If a dream promotes sin, pride, fear, or confusion, it is not from Him. The Bible is the final authority. The Holy Spirit confirms through Scripture.
2. ***Consider the Context of Your Life:*** Some dreams reflect stress, recent conversations, or daily thoughts. Not everything is spiritual warfare. Ask: Is this dream influenced by something I saw or thought about yesterday or recently?
3. ***Look for Christ-Centered Meaning:*** God's messages in dreams align with redemption, correction, direction, or warning; not superstition. In Scripture, dreams often prepared people for purpose (Joseph in Matthew 1–2). Christ remains central.

4. ***Seek Prayer and Wise Counsel:*** Joseph and Daniel interpreted dreams in humility. Avoid self-interpretation driven by emotion. Pray first. If necessary, seek mature counsel. Peace is a key indicator of God's voice.

Consider Pharaoh's dream (Genesis 41). The interpretation brought preparation, not panic. True divine revelation produces clarity and direction.

Dreams are not meant to control you. The Holy Spirit guides believers primarily through the Word and inner witness. Dreams are secondary, not foundational. So, do not fear dreams. Do not idolize them. Test them.

Christ is your Shepherd. He leads clearly.

Action: *If you have a troubling dream, write it down, pray over it, and measure it against Scripture before reacting.*

Let us pray

1. *Father, thank You that You speak clearly and faithfully, in Jesus' name.*
2. *Lord, deliver me from fear and confusion regarding dreams, in Jesus' name.*
3. *Holy Spirit, give me discernment to interpret correctly, in Jesus' name.*
4. *Father, align every revelation in my life with Your Word, in Jesus' name.*
5. *I decree that Christ leads me in clarity and truth, in Jesus' name.*

Sunday 17 May **A SWORD FOR BATTLE**

Read: Ephesians 6:10-17;
Hebrews 4:12

Bible in 1 year: Psa. 13-15
Bible in 2 years: Deut. 8-9

"And take the helmet of salvation, and the sword of the Spirit, which is the word of God" (Ephesians 6:17).

In spiritual warfare, the only offensive weapon listed in the armor of God is the sword of the Spirit – the Word of God. Shields defend. Helmets protect. But the sword advances. Without the Word, a believer stands armed yet unable to strike. Imagine a soldier well-equipped with bulletproof gadgets, but without a gun.

When Jesus was tempted in the wilderness, He did not argue with Satan. He did not display miracles. He said, "It is written." Three times He used Scripture as His weapon (Matthew 4:1–11). The Son of God chose the Word as His sword. If Christ relied on Scripture in battle, how much more should we?

A sword must be sharp and skillfully used. Owning a Bible is not the same as wielding it. The Word must be known, believed, spoken, and obeyed. Hebrews 4:12 declares that the Word of God is living and powerful – piercing, discerning, cutting through deception.

Consider a soldier entering battle without training in his weapon. Fear will dominate him. But when trained and confident, he advances boldly. Many believers are defeated not because they lack promises, but because they lack familiarity with them.

The sword is not for display; it is for engagement. When fear whispers, declare truth. When temptation rises, speak Scripture. When doubt attacks, proclaim God's promises.

At the Cross, Jesus secured victory. The Word enforces that victory daily. Enlargement requires spiritual precision. Casual Christianity produces dull blades. Consistent meditation produces sharpness.

Sharpen your sword through study and prayer. Keep it near your heart. Speak it with faith. Victory belongs to those who wield the Word.

Action: *Memorize one Scripture this week and use it intentionally in prayer and declaration.*

Let us pray

1. *Father, thank You for giving me Your living Word, in Jesus' name.*
2. *Lord, ignite hunger in me to study and meditate on Scripture, in Jesus' name.*
3. *Holy Spirit, teach me to wield the Word with boldness and accuracy, in Jesus' name.*
4. *Father, silence every lie of the enemy through Your truth, in Jesus' name.*
5. *I strike every satanic power challenging my destiny, and I recover all lost blessings, in Jesus' name.*

Monday 18 May

STRENGTH FOR THE BATTLE

Read: Ephesians 6:10–18

Bible in 1 year: Psa. 16-18
Bible in 2 years: Deut. 10-11

"Finally, my brethren, be strong in the Lord and in the power of His might." (Ephesians 6:10)

True strength in the midst of life's fiercest battles is never found in human resolve or psychological grit; it is found exclusively in the Lord. The Apostle Paul's exhortation in Ephesians 6:10 is a call to a specific posture: "be strong in the Lord." The Greek word *dynamis*, used here, refers to inherent power and divine ability. When the storms of life begin to rage, our natural resolve often snaps, but God's power within us is unbreakable. Strength is not the absence of trials or the avoidance of conflict; it is the presence of the Almighty's power residing within a human vessel, enabling us to stand firm when the world expects us to collapse.

Consider the life of David. In 1 Samuel 30, he returned to Ziklag to find his city burned, his family captured, and his own men speaking of stoning him. The text notes that David was "greatly distressed," yet he found strength in the Lord his God. David's victory did not begin when he defeated his enemies on the battlefield; it began when he turned to the Lord in the middle of his despair. This teaches us that the battle is won internally before it is ever fought externally. When you are strong in the Lord, you are not moved by the changing tides of circumstance because your foundation is the unshakeable character of God.

Are you attempting to fight your battles with your own limited resources? Many believers find themselves exhausted because they are trying to fix their problems with intellect, manipulation, or mere willpower. These are brittle tools in the face of spiritual warfare. Today, stop trying to be strong *for* the Lord and start being strong *in* the Lord. Let His inherent power become your armor. When you anchor yourself in His might, you discover a resilience that defies logic, allowing you to stand, withstand, and prevail even when the odds are stacked against you.

Prophetic Declaration: *I declare that I am strong in the Lord and in the power of His might! His strength sustains me, and I shall not be moved by any trial!*

Let us pray

1. *Lord, strengthen me today with Your mighty power, not my own failing efforts.*
2. *Grant me a resilient spirit that remains calm and steady in the face of difficult times.*
3. *Keep my faith unshaken, even when the storms of life seem to rage against me.*
4. *Empower me to stand firm in every battle, knowing that You are fighting on my behalf.*
5. *Let Your strength be perfected in my weakness, Lord; manifest Your power through me.*

Prophetic Prayer of the Week

1. ***"Stir up the gift of God which is in you." (2 Timothy 1:6).*** *My calling and spiritual mantle are activated today, in Jesus' name.*

2. ***"I have given you authority… over all the power of the enemy." (Luke 10:19).*** *My authority in Christ is restored, and every power of darkness bows, in Jesus' name.*
3. ***"For I know the plans I have for you." (Jeremiah 29:11)*** *God's plan and purpose for my life must come to pass, in Jesus' name.*

Tuesday 19 May

THE SPEED OF OBEDIENCE

Read: Psalm 119:57-64

Bible in 1 year: Psa. 19-21
Bible in 2 years: Deut. 12-13

"I made haste, and did not delay to keep Your commandments" (Psalm 119:60).

The prophetic instruction to "Enlarge the place of your tent" is not just an invitation; it is a time-sensitive command. After securing Divine Direction through our Intimacy with God, the decisive factor for manifestation is the speed of our obedience. Delay is often the spiritual gap that allows doubt, human reasoning, and the enemy's schemes to creep in and compromise the purity of the blueprint – divine direction received from God.

The Psalmist understood the urgency of obedience. He declared, *"I made haste, and did not delay to keep Your commandments."* Friend, God's timing is crucial in everything He wants to do in your life. Never forget that the resources, connections, and favor needed for your enlargement often appear within specific windows of opportunity. Discernment and timely obedience are therefore critical. When Elisha instructed the widow to go and borrow empty vessels and begin pouring the little oil she had (2 Kings 4:1–7), that instruction created a window for her miracle. Her breakthrough depended on acting immediately and in faith. Likewise, when Elijah asked the widow of Zarephath to prepare a meal for him with the very last portion of food she had (1 Kings 17:8–16), it was not merely a request; it was a divine opportunity for supernatural provision. By responding in faith rather than waiting for a more convenient moment, they entered into their season of divine supply.

Fasting and prayer help us build the spiritual muscle to respond to the Spirit's prompting with immediate, unquestioning action. Prayerlessness weakens your capacity to discern divine opportunities.

Do you want to experience divine interventions this year? You must guard against the subtle enemy called procrastination. This spirit manifests through fear or the desire to analyze God's command fully before obeying it. Friend, your assignment is not to understand every detail, but to trust God and make haste to obey His instructions.

Prompt obedience will strengthen your spiritual stakes and prove your reliability for the greater assignments God has for you this year. Let your motto today be: No Delay! Receive the command, and move swiftly to execute the divine strategy for your expanded territory.

Action: *Commit yourself today to obeying immediately and completely the very first clear, positive instruction or conviction you receive from the Holy Spirit, without delaying or rationalizing it.*

Let us pray

1. *Father, I thank You for the clear Divine Direction You have given me, in Jesus' name.*
2. *Holy Spirit, remove every spirit of procrastination, delay, and paralysis from my life, in Jesus' name.*
3. *I receive the grace to make haste and to be a swift, unquestioning doer of Your Word, in Jesus' name.*
4. *Lord, let my immediate obedience accelerate the manifestation and establishment of my Enlargement this year, in Jesus' name.*

5. *I declare that the time-sensitive opportunities for my breakthrough are seized with speed and precision, in Jesus' name.*

Wednesday 20 May

WAR AGAINST THE SPIRIT OF DELAY

Read: Daniel 10:12-13;
Joel 2:25-27

Bible in 1 year: Psa. 22-24
Bible in 2 years: Deut. 14-15

"Do not fear, Daniel, for from the first day... your words were heard" (Daniel 10:12).

Delay can be one of the most discouraging battles in a believer's life. You prayed. You fasted. You obeyed. Yet the answer seems postponed. Over time, hope weakens, and vision fades. But not every delay is denial.

In Daniel 10, the prophet fasted for twenty-one days. Heaven had responded from the first day, yet spiritual resistance hindered manifestation. The answer was sent, but warfare occurred in the unseen realm. This reveals that some delays are due to spiritual opposition that requires persistent prayer.

However, we must be careful. Not every delay is demonic. Some delays are divine preparation. Jesus delayed visiting Lazarus, yet that delay produced greater glory (John 11:6). Christ is never late; He operates on redemptive timing.

The spirit of delay seeks to produce frustration, doubt, and spiritual fatigue. It whispers, "It will never happen." If not confronted, it leads to compromise. Abraham and Sarah tried to help God through Hagar because the promise seemed delayed.

Warfare against delay involves persistence in prayer, alignment with God's will, and unwavering faith. Jesus taught that men ought always to pray and not lose heart (Luke 18:1). Persistence positions you for a breakthrough.

Consider a seed planted underground. For a season, nothing appears visible. Yet roots are developing. Delay is sometimes growth beneath the surface.

At the Cross, Jesus defeated every force assigned to obstruct destiny. Joel promises restoration of lost years. What seemed stalled can be accelerated by divine intervention.

Enlargement requires endurance. Refuse to surrender to discouragement. Stand firm in faith. God's timing is perfect, and His promise remains secure.

Action: *Identify one promise you have almost given up on and recommit it to persistent prayer.*

Let us pray

1. *Father, thank You that You hear me from the first day I pray, in Jesus' name.*
2. *Father, I break every satanic power and pattern assigned to delay my progress and destiny,* ***in Jesus' name.***
3. *Lord, arise and scatter every power and opposition standing on the road of my advancement,* ***in Jesus' name.***
4. *Father, restore every opportunity and season I lost through delay and grant me divine speed,* ***in Jesus' name.***
5. *Lord, give me sensitivity to recognize Your opportunities and the grace to obey quickly,* ***in Jesus' name.***

Thursday 21 May **THE POWER OF PERSISTENCE**

Read: Luke 18:1–8

Bible in 1 year: Eze. 22-24
Bible in 2 years: Deut. 16-17

"And will not God bring about justice for his chosen ones, who cry out to him day and night?" (Luke 18:7)

The parable of the persistent widow teaches that prayer is not always about convincing a reluctant God to act, but about maintaining our stance until the answer manifests. The widow's power did not come from her status or her legal arguments; it came from her refusal to quit. In a culture where she had no advocate, her sheer persistence became her greatest weapon.

Consider the story of George Müller, who cared for thousands of orphans in 19th-century England. Müller famously prayed for years for the salvation of five specific friends. One by one, they came to faith—the last one years after Müller had died. His persistence was not a sign of desperation; it was a sign of confident faith. He knew that if he kept bringing the matter before the Judge, the answer was inevitable.

When you pray, do you quit when the "door" remains closed for a week, a month, or a year? Persistence is the crucible of faith. It transforms a request into a conviction. Like the widow, we are called to bring our petitions to God, not as beggars, but as sons and daughters who know the Father hears.

Prophetic Declaration: *I will not grow weary in well-doing! My* *persistent prayers are releasing the hand of God! I shall see the justice of the Lord in the land of the living!*

Let us pray

1. *Father, give me the spirit of the persistent widow—a heart that refuses to lose hope.*
2. *Lord, help me to distinguish between waiting on Your timing and settling for the enemy's delays.*
3. *Holy Spirit, strengthen my hands and knees when the battle for my breakthrough gets weary.*
4. *O Lord, I bring my persistent requests before You today, trusting in Your faithful justice.*
5. *I receive the grace to stand firm, knowing that my persistent prayers are moving the mountains!*

Friday 22 May **ARE YOU SINNING DELIBERATELY?**

Read: Hebrews 10:26-29

Bible in 1 year: Eze. 25-27
Bible in 2 years: Deut. 18-19

"If we deliberately keep on sinning after we have received the knowledge of the truth, no sacrifice for sins is left" (Hebrews 10:26 NIV).

Sinning deliberately after knowing the truth is suicidal! Hebrews 10 confronts us with a thought-provoking truth: there is great danger in continuing to practice sin after God has revealed the truth of salvation. This is not about occasional failure or weakness, but about deliberate, habitual sin – choosing darkness while knowing the light.

In John 8:11, Jesus warned clearly, *"Go and sin no more."* Paul asked sharply, *"Shall we continue in sin that grace may abound? By no means!" (Romans 6:1-2).* Peter spoke just as strongly, saying it is worse to know the way of righteousness and turn back than never to have known it at all (2 Peter 2:20-21). Scripture agrees with one voice: truth demands transformation – change of lifestyle.

The Bible gives tragic examples of people who ignored God's warning. Samson continued in lust despite repeated deliverances until the Spirit departed, and he did not realize it (Judges 16:20). Judas walked with Jesus, heard truth daily, yet clung to the secret sin of theft until it was impossible for him to repent. Deliberate sin dulls the conscience, hardens the heart, and blurs the voice of the Holy Spirit.

In real life, we see similar patterns. A believer repeatedly warned about an immoral relationship, who chooses pleasure over obedience, ends in disaster. At first, there is conviction. Later, there is silence. Soon, prayer becomes empty, joy disappears, and faith grows cold. Sin always promises freedom but produces bondage.

Why does a believer continue in sin after warning? Often due to unchecked desires, fear of surrender, deception, or a lack of accountability. Sin thrives where light is avoided.

Freedom begins with honesty and repentance. Confession restores sensitivity. God's grace is powerful, but it must not be abused. The cross frees us not only from sin's penalty, but from its power. Grace teaches us to say NO to sin, not yes (Titus 2:11-12).

Ignoring conviction is like ignoring pain in the body. At first, it warns you. If ignored, damage deepens.

Action: *Ask the Holy Spirit to reveal to you any deliberate sin in your life. Repent, cut off access, and seek accountability today.*

Let us pray

1. *Father, thank You, Lord, for the truth that sets me free, in Jesus' name.*
2. *Lord, search my heart and expose any deliberate sin that has trapped me, in Jesus' name.*
3. *Father, restore sensitivity to Your Holy Spirit and the fear of God in my heart, in Jesus' name.*
4. *Fire of God, fall on me now, and break the power of habitual sin, in Jesus' name.*
5. *Lord, lead me daily and establish my feet on the path of obedience and holiness, in Jesus' name.*

Saturday 23 May

DON'T BE DECEIVED BY THE OCCULT

Read: Deuteronomy 18:10–12

Bible in 1 year: Eze. 28-30
Bible in 2 years: Deut. 20-21

"See to it that no one takes you captive through hollow and deceptive philosophy… rather than on Christ" (Colossians 2:8).

The occult often presents itself as harmless, spiritual, or enlightening. It promises hidden knowledge, protection, healing, or power. Yet behind the attractive appearance lies deception. What looks like light is actually darkness in disguise. Satan uses these practices as bait—offering quick answers and supernatural experiences—to pull people away from simple trust in God.

Many are trapped because the deception feels real. A horoscope seems accurate. A medium reveals personal details. A charm appears to "work." But even a small truth can be used to sell a big lie. The enemy mixes facts with falsehood to gain trust, then slowly leads a person into fear, bondage, and dependence on powers that are not from God. Instead of freedom, there is oppression. Instead of peace, there is anxiety.

Scripture clearly warns us not to consult divination, spirits, or magical practices. God forbids these things because He loves us and knows their danger. Occultism mimics God's power while cutting us off from His presence. It whispers, "You can control your destiny," feeding pride and self-deification, while Christ calls us to humble faith and surrender.

In Acts 19:19, new believers in Ephesus publicly burned their magic books after meeting Jesus. They chose freedom over fascination. Revival came when they renounced the occult completely.

Beloved, we do not need secret powers—we have the Holy Spirit. We do not need charms—we have Christ. True protection and guidance come only from God.

Action: *Remove and renounce every object or practice connected to the occult and commit fully to Christ alone.*

Let us pray

1. *Father, thank You for delivering me from every hidden snare of darkness, in Jesus' name.*
2. *Lord, expose and uproot every deception trying to enter my life, in Jesus' name.*
3. *Holy Spirit, fill me with discernment to reject every counterfeit power, in Jesus' name.*
4. *Father, break every chain of fear, oppression, or bondage from past involvement, in Jesus' name.*
5. *Lord Jesus, establish me in Your truth and keep me walking in Your light always, in Jesus' name.*

Sunday 24 May

OVERCOME THE VICTIM MENTALITY

Read: John 5:1-9

Bible in 1 year: Eze. 31-33
Bible in 2 years: Deut. 22-23

"Rise, take up your bed and walk" (John 5:8).

One of the most subtle toxic mentalities that hinders the progress of believers is the victim mentality. It says, *"It's not my fault. If others had helped me, I would be further or better."* It shifts responsibility outward and waits endlessly for change to come from people rather than from God.

In John 5, a man had been sick for thirty-eight years. When Jesus asked him, *"Do you want to be made well?"* his response was revealing: *"I HAVE NO MAN to put me into the pool."* He focused on who failed him rather than what God could do for him. His condition was real. His pain was real. But his mindset had settled into helplessness.

Jesus did not argue with his history. He gave him a command: "RISE." In that moment, Christ shifted him from victimhood to responsibility. Healing required participation. He had to stand.

Many believers remain stuck not because God has not spoken, but because they are rehearsing past injuries. They blame family background, church leadership, economy, or betrayal. While those factors may have influenced you, they do not define your destiny. Jesus does.

At the Cross, Christ absorbed injustice without adopting a victim identity. He suffered wrongfully, yet He entrusted Himself to the Father (1 Peter 2:23). If anyone had the right to claim victimhood, it was Jesus. Instead, He rose in victory.

Growth begins when you stop asking, "Who failed me?" and start asking, "Lord, what are You calling me to do now?" Healing flows when responsibility replaces blame.

Enlargement requires ownership. Christ calls you to rise above excuses. Your past may explain you, but it does not have permission to imprison your future.

Action: *Identify one area where you have been blaming others and take one responsible step toward change this week.*

Let us pray

1. *Father, thank You for the victory I have in Christ, in Jesus' name.*
2. *Lord, forgive me for blaming others instead of trusting You for my breakthrough, in Jesus' name.*
3. *Holy Spirit, empower me to rise above my past wounds, in Jesus' name.*
4. *Father, heal every area of injustice in my life and establish me in my purpose, in Jesus' name.*
5. *Father, you will help me as You have helped others; I step out today trusting Your support for excellent results in my work, in Jesus' name.*

Monday 25 May

BREAK THE POVERTY MINDSET

Read: 2 Corinthians 8:1-9

Bible in 1 year: Eze. 34-36
Bible in 2 years: Deut. 24-25

"For you know the grace of our Lord Jesus Christ, that though He was rich, yet for your sakes He became poor, that you through His poverty might become rich" (2 Corinthians 8:9).

The poverty mindset is not merely a lack of money; it is scarcity thinking. It says, *"There is never enough. I must hold tightly. I cannot risk giving."* It breeds fear, suspicion, and a small vision. Even when God provides, the heart remains anxious.

Paul speaks of the Macedonian believers who, though in deep poverty, flourished in generosity. They did not allow their circumstances to control their faith. Their mindset was shaped by grace, not scarcity.

At the center of our faith stands Jesus. Though rich in glory, He became poor for our sake. The Cross is the ultimate demonstration that heaven is not afraid to give. Christ did not cling to privilege; He released Himself in sacrificial generosity. When we focus on His love and example, the fear of lack begins to break from our hearts.

The poverty mindset limits growth by resisting obedience. It questions God's provision. It sees giving as loss rather than a seed – sowing. Consider the boy with five loaves of bread and two fish (John 6:9-13). If he had kept his meal in fear, thousands would have remained hungry. In

Christ's hands, little became abundance. The boy blessed multitudes and went home with more.

Scarcity thinking will shrink your destiny. But faith thinking will enlarge it. The issue is not how much you have, but how you see it. God multiplies the resources you have surrendered to him. Unfortunately, most people are blinded by the "Give me mindset."

Breaking the poverty mindset begins with gratitude, generosity, and trust. When Christ becomes your source, money loses its power to intimidate you. You move from survival to stewardship.

Enlargement requires a renewed perspective. The God who gave His Son will not abandon you. Reject fear and trust the God of the covenant. Live generously and enjoy the blessings of the Kingdom.

Action: *Prepare your heart and give out something for God's work you have not given before."*

Let us pray

1. *Father, thank You for being my unfailing source, in Jesus' name.*
2. *Lord, uproot every scarcity mentality from my heart, in Jesus' name.*
3. *Holy Spirit, teach me to trust Your provision fully, in Jesus' name.*
4. *Father, make me a channel of generosity and blessing, in Jesus' name.*
5. *Father, as I begin to sow sacrificially for your work, let me experience divine enlargement in every way this year, in Jesus' name.*

Prophetic Prayer of the Week

1. ***"It is He who gives power to get wealth." (Deuteronomy 8:18).*** *My prosperity is restored, and the work of my hands will flourish, in Jesus' name.*
2. ***"You anoint my head with oil." (Psalm 23:5).*** *The oil of the Holy Spirit is restored afresh upon my life, in Jesus' name.*
3. ***"The vision is yet for an appointed time." (Habakkuk 2:3).*** *Every delayed vision in my life is activated and accelerated, in Jesus' name.*

Tuesday 26 May

OVERCOME THE COMPARISON MENTALITY

Read: John 21:20–22;
Galatians 6:4–5

Bible in 1 year: Eze. 37-39
Bible in 2 years: Deut. 26-27

"What is that to you? You follow Me" (John 21:22).

The comparison mentality quietly poisons spiritual growth. It constantly measures personal progress against someone else's success. It whispers, *"Why not me? Why is their ministry growing faster? Why is their life easier?"* Comparison steals joy, distorts calling, and breeds insecurity.

After Jesus restored Peter, He spoke about Peter's future. But when Peter noticed John nearby, he asked, *"Lord, what about this man?"* Instead of concentrating on his own assignment, he shifted focus to John's destiny. Jesus replied firmly, *"What is that to you? You follow Me."*

That statement is liberating. Destiny is personal. Calling is specific. Comparison distracts from obedience.

Jesus never compared His disciples against each other. He did not tell Thomas to be like John, or John to be like Peter. Each was called uniquely. When comparison dominates, gratitude fades. You begin to undervalue what God has entrusted to you.

Consider two runners in a race. If one constantly turns to watch the other, he loses rhythm and speed. Focus determines finish.

The Cross reminds us that identity is secure in Christ, not in performance. God affirmed His Son before public miracles began: *"This is My beloved Son in whom I am well pleased" (Matthew 3:17).* Identity preceded activity. When your identity is rooted in Christ, comparison loses power.

Growth accelerates when you celebrate others and faithfully serve in your own lane. Enlargement happens when you follow Jesus fully, not competitively. If you keep looking sideways, you will miss what God is doing ahead. Christ's call remains simple and direct: Follow Me.

Action: *Celebrate someone else's success this week without comparing it to your own journey.*

Let us pray

1. *Father, thank You that my identity is secure in Christ, in Jesus' name.*
2. *Lord, forgive me for comparing myself with others, in Jesus' name.*
3. *Holy Spirit, teach me to celebrate others sincerely, in Jesus' name.*
4. *Father, help me focus on my unique calling, in Jesus' name.*
5. *Father, who I am is more important to You than what I do; help me to be before I do, in Jesus' name.*

Wednesday 27 May **SOME PEOPLE FEAR YOU**

Read: 1 Samuel 18:12-16

Bible in 1 year: Eze. 40-42
Bible in 2 years: Deut. 28

"Saul was afraid of David, because the Lord was with him but had departed from Saul" (1 Samuel 18:12).

Not everyone who smiles at you truly celebrates you. Sometimes, the reason people avoid, criticize, or fight you is not because you harmed them, but because God's hand is visible upon your life. Your progress, favor, and peace can quietly trouble those who lack God's presence.

David experienced this. He did nothing wrong to anyone. He served faithfully, defeated Goliath, and played music to soothe Saul. Yet Saul feared him. Why? *"The Lord was with him" (v.14).* God's presence with David exposed Saul's emptiness. Light naturally disturbs darkness.

Many believers become discouraged when they sense resistance or jealousy. They ask, "Why don't they like me?" But sometimes, it is not hatred; it is insecurity. Your discipline reminds them of their laziness. Your integrity exposes their compromise. Your prayer life unsettles their spiritual dryness and carnality.

Do not shrink yourself to make others comfortable. If God has blessed you, walk humbly but confidently. Jesus said, *"Let your light so shine before men" (Matthew 5:16).* Never dim your light to please fearful people.

At the same time, guard your heart. Don't become proud or suspicious. David never attacked Saul. He remained respectful and focused on God's assignment. When people fear you, respond with character, not revenge.

A young brother in the faith was mocked at work for refusing bribes. Later, when corruption was exposed, management trusted and promoted only him. The same people who despised him began to respect him. His integrity first created opposition, then honor.

If God is with you, some will fear you. Let that push you closer to God, not away from Him. Stay faithful. Your destiny is bigger than their opinion.

Action: *Examine your life today and commit to walking in humility and integrity without reducing your God-given light.*

Let us pray

1. *Father, let Your presence rest upon my life daily, in Jesus' name.*
2. *Lord, deliver me from the fear of people, in Jesus' name.*
3. *Holy Spirit, keep me humble as You bless me from glory to glory, in Jesus' name.*
4. *Father, defend me from jealousy and hidden attacks for those who fear You, in Jesus' name.*
5. *Lord, make my life a light that glorifies You everywhere I go, in Jesus' name.*

Thursday 28 May

BATTLE FOR FAMILY RECOVERY

Read: Isaiah 49:24-25;
Acts 16:31

Bible in 1 year: Eze. 43-45
Bible in 2 years: Deut. 29-30

"For I will contend with him who contends with you, and I will save your children" (Isaiah 49:25).

Total recovery is incomplete if it stops with you. God's covenant is generational. Yet many families battle repeated cycles – marital breakdown, addiction, poverty, anger, spiritual coldness. When patterns repeat across generations, warfare becomes necessary.

Isaiah asks, *"Shall the prey be taken from the mighty?"* Then God answers, *"Even the captives of the mighty shall be taken away."* This is divine assurance that no bondage is too strong for redemption.

In Acts 16, the Philippian jailer encountered Christ and was told, *"Believe on the Lord Jesus Christ, and you will be saved, you and your household."* Salvation was not meant to terminate at one life; it was designed to flow through families.

Generational warfare begins with personal alignment. Christ must first reign in your heart. You cannot break cycles you are still participating in. Repentance closes legal doors. Prayer establishes new spiritual patterns. The declaration of God's Word resets the atmosphere of a home and family

Consider Abraham. Though he came from an idolatrous background (Joshua 24:2), God called him out and established a new covenant line. One obedient decision shifted generational history.

The Cross speaks louder than inherited curses. Jesus became a curse for us (Galatians 3:13). Through His blood, old patterns lose authority. But believers must enforce that victory in prayer, teaching, and consistent example.

Enlargement includes family restoration. God desires households that reflect His glory.

Do not accept negative cycles as permanent. What has been running in your family can stop with you.

Action: *Pray intentionally this week for your family and speak deliverance and restoration over each family member.*

Let us pray

1. *Father, thank You for Your covenant over my family, in Jesus' name.*
2. *Lord, break every negative generational cycle limiting my family, in Jesus' name.*
3. *Holy Spirit, establish Christ at the center of my household, in Jesus' name.*
4. *Father, restore salvation, love, peace, and unity in my family, in Jesus' name.*
5. *Arise, O Father, let doors we have never known open to my family, in Jesus' name.*

Friday 29 May **5 WAYS ADULTERY DESTROYS A FAMILY**

Read: Proverbs 6:25-33

Bible in 1 year: Eze. 46-48
Bible in 2 years: Deut. 31

"Flee from sexual immorality. Every other sin a person commits is outside the body, but the sexually immoral person sins against his own body" (1 Corinthians 6:18).

Adultery is never a private sin. Though often hidden, its consequences ripple through marriages, children, and generations. Scripture speaks plainly about its danger because God designed the family to thrive in trust, faithfulness, covenant love, and purity. When adultery enters a home, it erodes foundations that take years to rebuild.

Here are five ways adultery destroys a family:

1. ***It Shatters Trust (Proverbs 6:32-33):*** Trust is the glue of marriage. Adultery breaks confidence between spouses, replacing safety with suspicion. Once trust is broken, every word and action is questioned, creating emotional distance and instability.
2. ***It Wounds Children Deeply (Malachi 4:6):*** Children may not know all the details, but they feel the tension. Adultery often leads to conflict, separation, or divorce, leaving children confused, insecure, and emotionally scarred.
3. ***It Invites Shame And Guilt Into The Home (Proverbs 5:9-11):*** Adultery brings hidden guilt to the one who falls and deep shame to the family. This burden affects communication, intimacy, and spiritual freedom.

4. ***It Destroys Intimacy And Unity (Genesis 2:24):*** Marital intimacy thrives on exclusivity and commitment. Adultery redirects affection and emotional energy outside the marriage, leaving the home cold and divided.
5. ***It Weakens Spiritual Authority And Legacy (1 Corinthians 6:18-19):*** Adultery grieves the Holy Spirit and weakens a family's spiritual foundation. Children raised in such pain may struggle to trust marriage, authority, and even God.

The Bible also presents to us a message of hope. God forgives the repentant, heals broken hearts, and restores what sin has damaged. While adultery may leave deep wounds, it does not have the final word over you. God can restore you and your marriage if you return to Him in repentance and humility.

Faithfulness in marriage is not merely a moral duty; it is a powerful act of love that protects your family and honors God. *"Blessed are the pure in heart, for they shall see God" (Matthew 5:8)*

Action: *Have you been unfaithful in any way? Seek repentance, accountability, and godly counsel, and commit afresh to walking in purity.*

Let us pray

1. *Father, I thank You for Your mercy, love, and faithfulness over my life and my family, in Jesus' name.*
2. *Lord, by the power of the blood of Jesus, deliver me and my household from every form of sexual sin and secret compromise, in Jesus' name.*
3. *God of restoration, heal every wound caused by unfaithfulness and rebuild trust, love, and peace in our home, in Jesus' name.*

4. *Holy Spirit, strengthen me to walk in purity, to guard my eyes and heart, and to overcome every temptation, in Jesus' name.*
5. *Lord, cleanse me as Your temple and restore spiritual authority in my family, establishing a godly legacy for the next generation, in Jesus' name.*

Saturday 30 May

RECLAIMING STOLEN TERRITORIES

Read: Obadiah 1:17; Joshua 1:3

Bible in 1 year: Col. 1-2
Bible in 2 years: Deut. 32

"But on Mount Zion there shall be deliverance... and the house of Jacob shall possess their possessions" (Obadiah 1:17).

There are territories in life that belong to you by divine promise but are not currently in your possession. There are also territories you have lost to the enemy. They may be areas of prayer consistency, moral discipline, financial order, leadership influence, family unity, spiritual authority, or family inheritance. Through negligence, sin, fear, or spiritual opposition, you surrendered ground to your enemy.

God told Joshua, *"Every place that the sole of your foot will tread upon I have given you."* Notice the tension: it was given, yet it had to be possessed. Promise does not eliminate warfare. Recovery requires courage.

In Christ, we have been seated in heavenly places (Ephesians 2:6). Authority has already been secured through the Cross. Colossians 2:15 declares that Jesus disarmed principalities and powers. Your victory is legal, but you must enforce it through vibrant faith and obedience.

Consider a landowner who legally owns property but allows intruders to occupy it. The title deed remains valid, yet possession is lost. Until he rises to reclaim it, others will misuse it. Many believers have legal victory but live below their inheritance.

Spiritual warfare is not shouting at the enemy without alignment; it is standing on truth, repenting where necessary, and boldly reclaiming your lost territory in Jesus' name. If your prayer life is weakened, rebuild it. If discipline has slipped, restore it. If your influence has declined, step forward again.

Enlargement requires recovery of lost ground. You cannot expand while retreating. Courage is the bridge between promise and possession.

Christ has already secured the territory. Your responsibility is to step forward and occupy.

Action: *Choose one area of your life where ground was lost and take a deliberate step to reclaim it this week.*

Let us pray

1. *Father, thank You for my victory over the devil secured through Christ, in Jesus' name.*
2. *Lord, forgive me for surrendering territory through fear or compromise, in Jesus' name.*
3. *Holy Spirit, strengthen me to stand boldly on Your promises and possess my possessions, in Jesus' name.*
4. *I rise by God's Word and begin to reclaim every lost territory in my life and family, in Jesus' name.*
5. *Father, let the angel of restoration visit my family and me this month for total recovery of lost territories, in Jesus' name.*

Sunday 31 May

BREAKING FORTH ON EVERY SIDE

Read: Isaiah 54:1–3

Bible in 1 year: Col. 3-4
Bible in 2 years: (Catch-up)

"For you shall expand to the right and to the left, and your descendants will inherit the nations, and make the desolate cities inhabited" (Isaiah 54:3).

God's promise of enlargement is never stagnant or confined; it is inherently expansive. When He speaks of breaking forth "to the right and to the left," He is describing a momentum that is essentially unstoppable. This breaking forth signifies that no barrier—whether economic, social, or spiritual—can effectively contain His people when He initiates their enlargement. History is filled with accounts of this supernatural progress. In the book of Joshua, the Israelites entered a land they did not cultivate and occupied cities they did not build. This was not the result of their military strategy, but the manifestation of God's promise to enlarge them beyond the limits of their own efforts.

This breaking forth is God's way of saying that your previous boundaries are no longer your final destination. Often, we define our potential by our past experiences or our current bank account, but divine enlargement is designed to shatter those narrow definitions. Think of a seed that has been underground for a season; when the right conditions arrive, it bursts through the soil. It doesn't just grow; it *breaks forth.* This is the season God is calling you into—a time where the barriers that have held your ministry, your career, or your family back are being dismantled by His power.

Are you still living within the perimeter of your old limitations? God is calling you to "lengthen your cords." This means you must start preparing for the expansion before it is fully visible. If you are praying for growth in your business, start putting systems in place to handle it. If you are praying for influence, start acting like someone who carries it. Breaking forth requires both faith and action. Today, identify one area where you desire to see this expansion and pray over it with a new level of expectation. You are not meant to stay small; you are meant to inherit and occupy.

Action: *Write down one specific area of your life where you desire enlargement (family, ministry, or career) and pray over it daily this week, declaring that God is removing the barriers.*

Let us pray

1. *Lord, cause me to break forth in every area of my life this year.*
2. *Expand my borders and enlarge the scope of my influence for Your Kingdom.*
3. *Let my life and my seed inherit new territories that were previously unreachable.*
4. *Remove every barrier—mental, physical, or spiritual—that hinders my enlargement.*

Make me fruitful and productive, even in places that were once desolate.

Read: Psalm 92:10–15; Matthew 25:1–13

Bible in 1 year: Matt. 1-4
Bible in 2 years: Deut. 33-34

"I have been anointed with fresh oil" (Psalm 92:10).

Oil in Scripture represents the anointing – the enabling presence of the Holy Spirit. Fresh oil speaks of renewed grace for present assignments. Yesterday's oil cannot sustain today's battles. When the anointing becomes stale through neglect, routine replaces power.

David declared, *"I shall be anointed with fresh oil."* Notice he did not rely on past victories. Though he had slain Goliath and survived Saul, he still needed fresh empowerment. Spiritual history does not guarantee present effectiveness.

In Matthew 25, the wise virgins carried extra oil; the foolish did not. When the bridegroom delayed, only those with oil were ready. Oil cannot be borrowed in critical moments. Intimacy cannot be outsourced. The anointing on you flows from your personal communion with God.

Sometimes we lose freshness through overexposure without refilling—preaching without praying, serving without resting in God, leading without lingering in His presence. Gradually, we function mechanically. The words may still be correct, but the weight of glory is missing.

Consider a lamp. If oil is not replenished, the flame flickers and eventually dies. The problem is not the wick; it is the supply. Many believers blame circumstances, but the deeper issue is dryness and negligence at the altar.

The good news is that fresh oil is available. Through Christ, the Anointed One, we have access to continual renewal. Isaiah 61 declares that He gives *"the oil of joy for mourning."* Recovery begins when we return to the secret place and invite the Holy Spirit to saturate us again.

Enlargement requires fresh grace. New levels demand new oil. Do not live on yesterday's encounters. Seek daily infilling. When the oil flows, strength returns, joy rises, and effectiveness increases. The God who anointed you before is ready to anoint you again.

Action: *Set aside extended time this week for worship and waiting on the Holy Spirit for renewal.*

Let us pray

1. *Father, thank You for the gift of the Holy Spirit, in Jesus' name.*
2. *Lord, forgive me for relying on past grace instead of seeking fresh oil, in Jesus' name.*
3. *Holy Spirit, refill and renew me with fresh anointing, in Jesus' name.*
4. *Father, remove dryness and restore spiritual vitality in my life, in Jesus' name.*
5. *I receive fresh oil for supernatural enlargement, in Jesus' name (Pray in tongues for at least 15 minutes).*

Prophetic Prayer of the Week

1. ***"Fan into flame the gift of God." (2 Timothy 1:6).*** *My prayer altar receives fresh fire, in Jesus' name.*

2. **The Lord turned the captivity of Job." (Job 42:10).** *Every captivity in my life is reversed, and my restoration begins, in Jesus' name.*
3. **"No weapon formed against you shall prosper." (Isaiah 54:17).** *My family is secured and every evil assignment against us fails, in Jesus' name.*

Tuesday 2 June

THE FIRE WE CANNOT IGNORE

Read: Acts 8:14–17; Acts 1:4–8

Bible in 1 year: Matt. 5-7
Bible in 2 years: Luke 1:1-38

"Then they laid hands on them, and they received the Holy Spirit." (Acts 8:17)

The early church understood a fundamental truth that many modern believers often overlook: receiving the Word of God is the beginning, but receiving the baptism in the Holy Spirit is the empowerment for the journey. When the apostles in Jerusalem heard that Samaria had received the Word, they did not stop at celebration; they sent Peter and John to pray that the new believers might receive the Holy Spirit. This was not merely a ceremonial act; it was a recognition that without the Spirit's fire, missions become mere human effort. Jesus Himself was explicit in Acts 1:8, stating that power is received *when* the Holy Spirit comes upon us, and that this power is the catalyst for our witness.

Without this baptism, our service often lacks the spiritual impact required to break chains or penetrate hearts. We might have the right theology, the best intentions, and even natural talent, but we lack the supernatural "fire" that makes a witness effective. Consider the radical transformation of Peter. Before Pentecost, he was paralyzed by the fear of man, even denying Christ to a servant girl. Yet, after being filled with the Spirit, he stood before the very crowds that had condemned Jesus and preached with such authority that 3,000 souls were saved in a single day. The difference was not a change in his education or his personality—it was the baptism of the Holy Spirit.

Are you attempting to live a supernatural life with natural resources? It is time to stop settling for the "Word" alone and pursue the "Power." The baptism in the Spirit is not a historical artifact or an optional upgrade for the elite; it is the essential fuel for every child of God who intends to be a witness. As you engage in your daily assignments, do not rely on your own strength. Seek the Holy Spirit's empowerment, for He is the one who transforms our weak efforts into manifestations of God's Kingdom.

Action: *Set aside time today to pray specifically for a fresh baptism in the Holy Spirit, asking Him to empower your witness and purge any reliance on self.*

Let us pray

1. *Lord, awaken in me a desperate urgency for the baptism of the Holy Spirit.*
2. *Fill me afresh with Your power so that my witness carries divine authority.*
3. *Deliver me from the trap of relying on my human talent for Your work.*
4. *Let my life be marked by supernatural elevation and spiritual impact.*
5. *Unite us as one body, ignited by the same fire of the Holy Spirit.*

Wednesday 3 June

THE EVIDENCE OF THE SPIRIT'S BAPTISM

Read: Acts 4:29–31;
1 Corinthians 12:7–11

Bible in 1 year: Matt. 8-11
Bible in 2 years: Luke 1:39-80

"And when they had prayed, the place where they were assembled together was shaken; and they were all filled with the Holy Spirit, and they spoke the word of God with boldness." (Acts 4:31)

When the Holy Spirit baptizes a believer, transformation is not just a possibility; it is an inevitable outcome. The immediate evidence in the early church was a shift from fear to supernatural boldness. In Acts 4, the believers did not pray for the persecution to stop; they prayed for the courage to continue. When they were filled, the environment shook, and their words gained a piercing, revelatory power. As Paul writes in 1 Corinthians 12:7, the manifestation of the Spirit is given to each one for the profit of all. This baptism is never just for personal gratification; it is the engine of collective empowerment.

Mark 16:17–18 declares that signs will follow those who believe, including healing, deliverance, and authority over the kingdom of darkness. These are the markers of a Spirit-filled mission. Think of the Apostle Paul and Barnabas in Acts 13:2–3; their mission was elevated from simple regional ministry to a global movement because they operated under the specific set-apart leading of the Spirit.

Consider the practical example of a timid believer who struggled for years to share their faith due to rejection anxiety. After a true encounter with the baptism of the Spirit, their timidity was replaced by a spirit of power, and their testimony became a primary instrument for leading others to Christ.

If you desire to see the "signs" of the Kingdom in your life, you must value the "Spirit" of the Kingdom. Boldness, the release of spiritual gifts, and a heightened sensitivity to God's voice are the hallmarks of a Spirit-baptized life. Today, acknowledge that you have been called to profit others through the gifts God has placed within you. Do not let your testimony be hidden by fear; let the fire of the Spirit purge your insecurities and turn your natural weakness into supernatural strength.

Prophetic Declaration: *I declare that I am baptized in the Holy Spirit! Boldness, gifts, and supernatural signs follow me! My life and mission are elevated by His power, and nothing shall be impossible!*

Let us pray

1. *Lord, let a new level of holy boldness rise in me through the power of Your Spirit.*
2. *Release the gifts You have placed in me for the profit of the Body of Christ.*
3. *Confirm Your Word in my life with supernatural signs and wonders.*
4. *Elevate me in my mission by Your direct, unmistakable leading.*
5. *Make me an effective vessel for healing, deliverance, and restoration.*

Thursday 4 June

BORN OF THE SPIRIT

Read: John 3:1–8

Bible in 1 year: Matt. 12-15
Bible in 2 years: Luke 2

"Most assuredly, I say to you, unless one is born again, he cannot see the kingdom of God" (John 3:3).

When Jesus spoke to Nicodemus, a man steeped in religious tradition and moral correctness, He introduced a concept that defied natural logic: the necessity of being "born again." This was not a call to improve one's behavior or attend more temple services; it was a demand for a fundamental, spiritual metamorphosis. Jesus explained that while we are born of the flesh, we must also be born of the Spirit. As He noted in John 3:6, "That which is born of the flesh is flesh, and that which is born of the Spirit is spirit." Regeneration is the work of the Holy Spirit, who bridges the gap between our fallen nature and the divine life of God.

This new birth is the absolute prerequisite for entering the Kingdom. Titus 3:5 reinforces this, describing it as the "washing of regeneration and renewing of the Holy Spirit." This is not a static event that occurs once and remains in the past; it is the beginning of a living, ongoing connection. Think of a seed planted in the soil. The transformation that happens underground is invisible at first, but it changes the very nature of the seed, allowing it to sprout into a new plant. Similarly, regeneration fundamentally alters our DNA in Christ, enabling us to perceive the things of God that were once hidden to us.

Many believers struggle with repetitive sin because they try to manage their "old self" rather than walking in the reality of their "new self." You were not created to simply manage your fleshly urges; you were created to live from the power of the Spirit who lives within you. The power that raised Jesus from the dead is the same power that is currently working in your life to renew your mind. Today, stop viewing your faith as a set of rules to follow. Recognize that you are a vessel of the living Spirit, being renewed day by day, and allow that truth to govern your thoughts and actions.

Action: *Ask the Holy Spirit today to identify one area of your life that still operates on "fleshly" power, and intentionally surrender that area for a fresh "renewal" by the Spirit.*

Let us pray

1. *Lord, thank You for the miracle of my new birth and the gift of the Holy Spirit.*
2. *Renew my mind daily, Lord, so that I may fully walk in the reality of being a new creation.*
3. *Deliver me from the power of the flesh and help me to yield to Your Spirit instead.*
4. *Keep me intimately connected to You through the ongoing work of regeneration.*
5. *Let this new life in me grow and manifest in my character every single day.*

Friday 5 June **NEW LIFE IN THE SPIRIT**

Read: Galatians 5:16–25

Bible in 1 year: Matt. 16-19
Bible in 2 years: Luke 3; 4:1-21

"If we live in the Spirit, let us also walk in the Spirit" (Galatians 5:25).

Paul the Apostle makes it clear that the Christian life is not defined by the weight of our self-effort, but by -the fruit of the Holy Spirit. In Galatians 5, he contrasts the "works of the flesh" with the "fruit of the Spirit"—love, joy, peace, longsuffering, kindness, goodness, faithfulness, gentleness, and self-control. The distinction here is crucial: works are what we produce through human exertion, while fruit is what grows naturally when we abide in the life-giving vine of the Spirit. Just as a branch does not strain to produce fruit, a believer does not need to force Christ-likeness through religious performance. We simply stay attached to the source, and His life flows through us.

This process is a dynamic journey of "walking." When Paul says to "walk in the Spirit," he is using the Greek word *stoicheo*, which implies marching in a line or following a set order. It requires an intentional, daily choice to stay in step with the Holy Spirit rather than drifting back into the independent patterns of our old nature. For example, consider the virtue of patience. When we are stuck in traffic or dealing with a difficult coworker, our natural instinct is frustration. However, when we are "walking" in the Spirit, we allow the Spirit's nature to supersede our natural reaction, replacing our irritation with a supernatural calm that is not our own.

If you find yourself constantly striving to be a "better person" but failing, perhaps you are trying to manufacture fruit without tending to the root. Our role is not to force change; our role is to yield. Today, practice the art of surrender. Before you speak, pause and ask the Spirit to guide your words. Before you react to pressure, ask the Spirit to cultivate self-control within you. When you live in the Spirit, the fruit will inevitably appear, because the life of Christ is inherently productive.

Prophetic Declaration: *I declare that I am a new creation, bearing the fruit of the Spirit, and walking in His power! I do not strive; I abide, and Christ's nature manifests through me!*

Let us pray

1. *Lord, let Your Spirit bear His beautiful fruit through my life today.*
2. *Transform my character into the likeness of Jesus, regardless of my circumstances.*
3. *Deliver me from all fleshly desires that hinder the growth of Your Spirit in me.*
4. *Teach me to walk in step with the Holy Spirit in every moment of this day.*
5. *Make my life a clear, undeniable testimony of Your love, peace, and goodness.*

Saturday 6 June **HEART BEFORE HANDS**

Read: Exodus 33:7–11

Bible in 1 year: Matt. 20-22
Bible in 2 years: Luke 4:22-44; 5

"The Lord would speak to Moses face to face, as one speaks to a friend." (Exodus 33:11)

Moses was a renowned leader, prophet, and miracle worker, yet his true distinction lay not in his public talent but in his private time with God. He established a "tent of meeting" outside the camp—a deliberate space where he withdrew from the clamor of leadership to commune with the Lord. Scripture records that God spoke to him "face to face," an intimacy born not of innate ability, but of consistent availability. While Israel admired the results of Moses' leadership, God valued the sincerity of Moses' presence.

The Hebrew word for "face" used in this passage is *panim*, which also translates to "presence". This teaches us that spiritual authority flows from lingering in God's presence, not from administrative skill or tactical brilliance. In our modern lives, it is easy to pour all our energy into "doing"—singing, preaching, or organizing—while neglecting the quiet "tent" of intimacy. Talent may open doors before men, but it is time spent with the Father that opens the heavens. Service that does not spring from this secret fellowship eventually runs dry.

Joshua, Moses' assistant, provides a striking example of this priority. Even after Moses left the tent to return to the camp, the young Joshua remained behind, lingering in the divine Presence. His future leadership of the nation was not shaped by a sudden promotion, but by the years he spent prioritizing God above all else. Are you the kind of believer who rushes back to the "camp" of activity the moment your religious duties are done? Time in God's presence restores lost strength. God raises leaders from those who find it hard to leave His feet.

Prophetic Declaration: *I declare that my life will be marked by presence, not performance! As I spend quality time with the Lord, He will shape my destiny and cause His glory to rest upon me.*

Let us pray

1. *Lord, teach me to value Your presence far above my natural abilities and talents.*
2. *Father, help me to build a "tent of meeting" in the middle of my busy daily schedule.*
3. *O Lord, let my strength and authority flow from intimacy with You, not from my performance.*
4. *Holy Spirit, deliver me from the pride of relying on my gifts without spending time in Your Presence.*
5. *I receive the grace to become a true friend of God through consistent, quiet fellowship.*

Sunday 7 June **REPENTANCE: THE TURNING POINT**

Read: Acts 3:19–21; 2 Peter 3:9

Bible in 1 year: Matt. 23-25
Bible in 2 years: Luke 6

"Repent therefore and be converted, that your sins may be blotted out, so that times of refreshing may come from the presence of the Lord." (Acts 3:19)

Repentance is frequently misidentified as a mere emotional response—a feeling of regret or sorrow over a mistake. However, biblically, repentance is a radical, deliberate "about-face." It is the act of turning away from the trajectory of sin and anchoring one's life toward God. Peter's urgent exhortation in Acts 3:19 links this turning directly to the arrival of "times of refreshing." This shows us that our internal struggles, dryness, and spiritual stagnation are often held in place by unconfessed or unabandoned sin. When we stop turning *toward* ourselves and start turning *toward* God, the atmosphere of our lives shifts.

God's heart regarding this is laid bare in 2 Peter 3:9: He is patient, not willing that any should perish, but that all should come to repentance. This tells us that repentance is not a hurdle God puts in our way to punish us; it is a doorway He opens to save us. It is an acknowledgment of our total inability to fix our own mess, which immediately invites the inflow of God's strength. Without repentance, sin remains like a wall between us and our blessing. With repentance, the blood of Jesus acts like a cleansing tide, blotting out the past and restoring our access to the Father's presence.

Are you living in a state of spiritual fatigue? Perhaps you are trying to "add" more religious activity to a life that is still harboring disobedience. True power cannot coexist with compromise. Today, be honest with the Lord. Repentance is not a sign of weakness; it is the strongest posture a human can take. It declares that you value the presence of the King more than the passing pleasures of the flesh. As you turn to Him, expect a refreshing that only the Lord can provide.

Prophetic Declaration: *I declare that as I repent, my sins are blotted out, and times of refreshing flow from the Lord into my life! I am clean, restored, and aligned with His purpose!*

Let us pray

1. *Lord, grant me a truly repentant heart that sees sin as You see it.*
2. *Help me to turn away from every habit that hinders my walk with You.*
3. *Blot out my past mistakes and failures by Your abundant mercy.*
4. *Refresh my weary soul with the glory of Your presence.*
5. *Keep me humble and dependent on You, far from the pride of self-righteousness.*

Monday 8 June

CONFESSION: THE LIVING TESTIMONY

Read: Romans 10:8–13

Bible in 1 year: Matt. 26-28
Bible in 2 years: Luke 7

"That if you confess with your mouth the Lord Jesus and believe in your heart that God has raised Him from the dead, you will be saved." (Romans 10:9)

Confession is far more than a simple vocalization; it is the outward seal of an inward transformation. Paul's instruction in Romans 10:9-10 bridges the gap between the private belief in our hearts and the public reality of our lives. In the early church, to confess "Jesus is Lord" was a dangerous, revolutionary act of allegiance. It meant declaring that Caesar was not the ultimate authority, which often led to severe persecution. Today, our confession remains a vital pillar of our walk with God. It is a declaration that shifts our allegiance from the kingdoms of this world to the Kingdom of God.

We must understand that confession is a living testimony. It is not a one-time magical formula that we recite once and then ignore. It is a continuous orientation of our lives. When we confess Jesus as "Lord," we are saying that He occupies the throne of our daily decisions, our finances, our relationships, and our secret thoughts. As 1 Corinthians 15:6 reminds us, the resurrection was witnessed by hundreds of people; our confession is our way of joining that cloud of witnesses, affirming that we serve a living Savior. A confession that does not affect our lifestyle is merely a hollow religious ritual.

How does your daily life "confess" the Lordship of Jesus? If your words claim He is Lord, but your choices reflect the values of the world, your confession is losing its power. Real confession seals our faith before God and acts as a beacon to a lost world. Today, examine your heart and your mouth. Are they in alignment? When you boldly declare Jesus as Lord, you are placing yourself under His protection and His mandate. Let your testimony be a living, breathing reality that others can see and, through your witness, desire to know for themselves.

Prophetic Declaration: *I declare that Jesus is Lord, risen from the dead! My confession seals my salvation, and my life is a living testimony to His reign in my heart!*

Let us pray

1. *Lord, strengthen my confession of faith in a world that pressures me to compromise.*
2. *Help me to boldly declare Jesus as Lord in my actions, my speech, and my private decisions.*
3. *Let my life be a living testimony that draws those around me to Your light.*
4. *Keep my heart and my mouth in perfect alignment with Your truth.*
5. *Make me a bold witness of Your resurrection power every day.*

Prophetic Prayer of the Week

1. ***"The yoke shall be destroyed because of the anointing." (Isaiah 10:27).*** *Every satanic embargo against my progress is broken, in Jesus' name.*
2. ***"They that wait upon the Lord shall renew their strength." (Isaiah 40:31).*** *My strength is renewed, and I rise above weakness, in Jesus' name.*

3. **"The Lord will give what is good." (Psalm 85:12).** *Every good thing delayed in my life is released, in Jesus' name.*

Tuesday 9 June **NEW SHOES**

Read: Ephesians 6:13–15; Joshua 1:3

Bible in 1 year: Heb. 1-4
Bible in 2 years: Luke 8

"And having shod your feet with the preparation of the gospel of peace" (Ephesians 6:15).

Shoes in Scripture often symbolize readiness, direction, and movement. You do not wear shoes to remain seated; you wear them to walk. Spiritually, "new shoes" speak of new seasons, new assignments, and fresh territory.

When God delivered Israel from Egypt, He instructed them to eat the Passover with sandals on their feet (Exodus 12:11). Why? Because freedom required movement. Deliverance was not the end – it was the beginning of a journey.

In Ephesians 6, Paul describes the armor of God and says our feet must be fitted with readiness. Shoes represent preparation. You cannot advance into new ground barefoot. Enlargement requires equipment.

Joshua stood at the edge of the Promised Land after Moses' death. God told him, *"Every place that the sole of your foot will tread upon I have given you."* The promise existed, but possession required stepping forward. New territory demands new steps.

Sometimes, believers pray for enlargement but resist change. We want a bigger territory without a new movement. But God does not give new shoes for decoration. He gives them for transition.

Consider a runner preparing for a marathon. Old, worn-out shoes cannot carry him through a long race. He needs fresh equipment for a new distance. In the same way, yesterday's mindset, habits, or spiritual discipline may not sustain tomorrow's assignment.

At the center of our walk is Christ. He directs our steps (Psalm 37:23). When He prepares new shoes, He prepares new grace. Your responsibility is obedience.

If God is giving you "new shoes," it means movement is coming. Do not fear transition. The One who equips your feet also goes before you.

Enlargement begins with a step.

Action: *Ask God where He is calling you to step forward in faith and take one practical action this week.*

Let us pray

1. *Father, thank You for preparing me for new seasons, in Jesus' name.*
2. *Lord, remove fear of transition and change from my heart, in Jesus' name.*
3. *Holy Spirit, direct my steps into divine purpose, in Jesus' name.*
4. *Father, equip me with grace for every new assignment, in Jesus' name.*
5. *Arise and do a prophetic walk, declaring, "I step higher into new territories, in Jesus' name."*

Wednesday 10 June

THE REWARD OF RELATIONSHIP

Read: John 15:4–8

Bible in 1 year: Heb. 5-7
Bible in 2 years: Luke 9

"Remain in me, as I also remain in you. No branch can bear fruit by itself; it must remain in the vine." (John 15:4)

In the vineyard, a branch does not struggle to produce fruit; it simply stays attached to the vine. The fruit is the natural byproduct of the sap flowing from the vine into the branch. We often confuse fruitfulness with striving, believing that if we work harder, pray longer, or organize better, we will produce more for the Kingdom. However, Jesus identifies the secret as *abiding* (remaining).

Think of an electronic device connected to a power source. It functions perfectly as long as it is plugged in; when it is unplugged, it eventually goes dark, regardless of how "capable" it is. Similarly, many believers operate on the residual "battery life" of past spiritual encounters, slowly dimming as they distance themselves from the source.

Consider the life of the Apostle John. He is famously known as the *"disciple whom Jesus loved"* (John 13:23). His proximity to Jesus was not just physical; it was relational. While others focused on who would be the greatest in the Kingdom, John focused on resting his head against the Master's chest. This relationship was the engine of his fruitfulness, enabling him to write the most profound theological insights about the nature of God's love.

Are you experiencing the joy of a life that bears fruit

naturally, or are you feeling the exhaustion of a life that is merely striving? True productivity is not about what you can manufacture through effort, but what God can manifest through you.

Prophetic Declaration: *I am a fruitful branch! I abide in Christ! The life of Christ flows through me, and I shall bear fruit that remains!*

Let us pray

1. *Father, teach me how to remain in You, even in the middle of a busy day.*
2. *Lord, deliver me from the exhaustion of striving and help me to rest in Your grace.*
3. *Holy Spirit, let the "sap" of Your life flow into every branch of my daily activities.*
4. *O Lord, prune away the dead weight in my life that keeps me from bearing true fruit.*
5. *I declare that I am attached to the Vine, and my life will be a constant display of Your fruitfulness!*

Read: Numbers 3:2–10

Bible in 1 year: Heb. 8-10
Bible in 2 years: Luke 10

"You shall appoint Aaron and his sons, and they shall attend to their priesthood; but the outsider who comes near shall be put to death" (Numbers 3:10).

God is particular about how He is served. In Numbers 3, the sons of Aaron were separated to minister with their father in the priesthood. Ministry was not casual volunteering; it was a sacred trust. They were called, appointed, and trained to handle holy things. God required order, purity, and obedience.

Yet Nadab and Abihu later offered "strange fire" before the Lord (Leviticus 10:1–2). It was a fire God had not commanded. Whether it came from rebellion, carelessness, or poor mentorship, the result was the same – unacceptable worship. Sincerity could not replace obedience. Strange fire is any service done God's way, replaced with our own way.

Today, we are God's priests (1 Peter 2:9). But we, too, can offer strange fire through preaching without prayer, ministry without consecration, charisma without character, emotional excitement without God's presence, or stepping into roles without preparation and submission. When we rush ahead without being trained, accountable, or spiritually disciplined, we bring human energy instead of holy fire.

The sons of Aaron remind us that calling alone is not enough. We need mentorship, instruction, and daily consecration. God does not just want activity on the altar; He wants purity on the altar.

Faithful priests guard their hearts, stay under authority, learn patiently, and depend on the Holy Spirit. The fire must come from God, not from the flesh. If the fire did not start in God's presence, it does not belong on God's altar.

Action: *Examine your service this week and remove anything done in self-effort; commit to prayer, accountability, and obedience before ministry.*

Let us pray

1. *Father, purify my heart and remove every strange fire from my service, in Jesus' name.*
2. *Lord, teach me to serve You according to Your Word and not my emotions, in Jesus' name.*
3. *Holy Spirit, train and mentor me to handle sacred responsibilities faithfully, in Jesus' name.*
4. *Father, deliver me from pride, haste, and careless ministry, in Jesus' name.*
5. *Lord, let Your holy fire alone burn continually upon the altar of my life, in Jesus' name.*

Friday 12 June

FREE FROM THE ENTITLEMENT MENTALITY

Read: Luke 15:11–24;
Philippians 2:5–8

Bible in 1 year: Heb. 11-13
Bible in 2 years: Luke 11

"Let this mind be in you which was also in Christ Jesus" (Philippians 2:5).

The entitlement mentality says, *"I deserve more. I should be recognized. I should be promoted."* It quietly feeds pride and resentment. When expectations are not met, offense grows. This mindset resists correction and avoids humble service, yet it cripples spiritual maturity.

In Luke 15, the prodigal son demanded his inheritance before time. He felt entitled to what was not yet due. His impatience led him to waste and loss. Entitlement made him blind to responsibility. Only when he came to himself and recognized his need did restoration begin.

In Philippians 2:5-8, Jesus presents the opposite spirit. Though equal with God, He did not cling to status. Instead, He humbled Himself, taking the form of a servant. The King of glory washed people's dirty feet. He chose obedience over privilege. At the Cross, He surrendered His rights for our redemption.

Entitlement suffocates gratitude. It makes blessings feel insufficient and service feel optional. A believer governed by the spirit of entitlement struggles with submission, generosity, and perseverance. Growth stops where pride settles.

Consider two employees: one works gratefully and happily, seeing opportunity; the other complains constantly about what he "deserves." Over time, the grateful one grows in trust and influence, while the entitled one stagnates.

In Christ, we receive grace, not wages. Everything we have is mercy. When we remember that salvation itself is undeserved, humility grows naturally. Promotion in God's kingdom follows humility, not demand.

Enlargement requires a servant's heart. When entitlement dies, gratitude lives. When pride bows, grace flows. Friend, true greatness is found in Christlike humility.

Action: *Serve someone intentionally this week without expecting recognition or reward.*

Let us pray

1. *Father, thank You for the grace I do not deserve, in Jesus' name.*
2. *Lord, uproot every spirit of pride and entitlement from my heart, in Jesus' name.*
3. *Holy Spirit, teach me to walk in humility like Christ, in Jesus' name.*
4. *Father, help me serve faithfully without seeking applause, in Jesus' name.*
5. *I receive divine power to serve people more, in Jesus' name.*

Saturday 13 June **BREAK THE COMFORT-ZONE MENTALITY**

Read: Matthew 14:22–33; Genesis 12:1–4

Bible in 1 year: Num. 1-3
Bible in 2 years: Luke 12

"And Peter answered Him and said, 'Lord, if it is You, command me to come to You on the water.' So He said, 'Come.'" (Matthew 14:28–29).

The comfort-zone mentality says, *"This is enough. I don't want to stretch. I don't want risk."* It prefers safety over growth, routine over obedience, and familiarity over faith. While comfort feels secure, it often becomes a cage.

In Matthew 14, the disciples were in a boat during a storm. The boat represented safety and control. But when Peter saw Jesus walking on the water, something within him longed for more. At Christ's command, he stepped out. The miracle was not in the boat; it was outside it.

Growth always requires movement. Abraham had to leave Ur before he could become the father of nations. If he had chosen familiarity over faith, his destiny would have stagnated.

Comfort zones are subtle. They appear reasonable. "I have done enough." "This level is fine." "Why stretch further?" Yet enlargement demands courage. You cannot possess new territory while refusing new obedience.

Consider a muscle. Without resistance, it weakens. With exercise, it grows stronger. Faith works the same way. If never stretched, it stagnates.

Jesus never called us His followers to convenience. He called us to follow Him. The Cross itself was the ultimate step outside comfort. Christ embraced obedience despite suffering. Because He stepped out, we stepped into salvation.

When you remain in your comfort zone, you avoid failure, but you also avoid growth. When you respond to Christ's "Come," you discover new dimensions of grace.

Enlargement lives beyond comfort. The Savior is not in the boat of safety; He is on the waters of faith. Step out now!

Action: *Take one faith-driven step this week that stretches you beyond familiarity. Do something you have not done before.*

Let us pray

1. *Father, thank You for calling me to growth and enlargement, in Jesus' name.*
2. *Lord, forgive me for choosing comfort over obedience, in Jesus' name.*
3. *Holy Spirit, give me courage to step out in faith, in Jesus' name.*
4. *Father, strengthen me to trust You beyond familiarity, in Jesus' name.*
5. *Father, as I step out of my comfort zone in obedience and faith, establish me in divine enlargement, in Jesus' name.*

Sunday 14 June

FAITHFULNESS IN LITTLE THINGS

Read: Luke 16:10–13

Bible in 1 year: Exo. 14-17
Bible in 2 years: Luke 13-14

"He who is faithful in what is least is faithful also in much; and he who is unjust in what is least is unjust also in much." (Luke 16:10)

The principle of faithfulness is the hidden foundation of all lasting growth. We often dream of "much"—more responsibility, more influence, and more resources—but God tests our readiness for "much" in the arena of the "least." The way you handle a small assignment is a prophetic indicator of how you will handle a grand mandate. If you are sloppy with your time, your finances, or your relationships now, you have no guarantee that you will be a better steward when you are given more. Faithfulness is not about the size of the task; it is about the posture of the heart.

This principle is the key to sustainable enlargement. God is not looking for people who are talented and flashy; He is looking for people who are reliable and steady. When you demonstrate faithfulness in the mundane, unseen tasks, you are building the spiritual muscle required for the burdens of leadership and expansion. Jesus emphasized that our attitude toward the "least" reveals our true character. Are you honoring your commitments, even when no one is cheering? Are you being a good steward of the small gifts you currently have?

Do not despise your day of small beginnings. The

work you are doing right now is the training ground for the greater assignments God has already set for your future. If you feel like your current situation is beneath your potential, change your perspective. See it as a test. Today, bring your best to everything you touch. Whether you are cleaning a desk, completing a report, or serving in your church, do it with excellence. As you prove faithful in the small things, God will surely trust you with much more. You are not waiting for an opportunity; you are creating one through your character.

Action: *Identify one small area of your life or work that you have been neglecting or treating with carelessness. Take steps to organize it and bring it to a level of excellence today.*

Let us pray

1. *Lord, help me to be a faithful steward of the small things You have entrusted to me.*
2. *Remove any desire for "more" that causes me to neglect the tasks I have now.*
3. *Transform my character, Lord, so that my life reflects Your excellence in every detail.*
4. *Grant me the discipline to remain consistent, especially when no one is watching.*
5. *Prepare my heart, Lord, so that I am ready for the "much" You are about to release.*

Monday 15 June **KEEP YOUR PROMISES**

Read: 1 Samuel 1:19-28

Bible in 1 year: Exo. 18-20
Bible in 2 years: Luke 15-16

"When you make a vow to God, do not delay to pay it… pay what you have vowed" (Ecclesiastes 5:4).

Many people make promises easily but fulfill them slowly, or not at all. We promise God faithfulness in prayer, service, or giving. We promise people help, support, or commitment. Yet when the cost becomes high, we withdraw. But God calls this unfaithfulness. *"It is required in stewards that one be found faithful" (1 Corinthians 4:2).*

Imagine if God stopped keeping His promises. The sun would not rise. Salvation would not be secure. Hope would collapse. God is faithful, and He expects His children to reflect His character.

Hannah teaches us true faithfulness. In her pain, she vowed, *"Lord, if You give me a son, I will give him back to You" (1 Samuel 1:11).* God answered. But now the test began. After years of waiting, she finally held Samuel in her arms. Every mother understands that bond. Yet when he was weaned, Hannah brought him to the temple and left him with Eli (v. 27–28). She kept her word.

How many would do that? It is easy to promise in desperation, but hard to fulfill in blessing. Yet obedience unlocks greater favor. After honoring her vow, *"the Lord visited Hannah… and she bore three sons and two daughters" (1 Samuel 2:21).* By keeping her promise, she opened the door for more.

Others did the same: Abraham offered Isaac, and God provided (Genesis 22:1–12). The danger of breaking vows is serious: *"It is better not to vow than to vow and not pay"* (Ecclesiastes 5:5).

Faithfulness builds trust with God and with people. If you break promises, even your children may struggle to trust you. Keep your word. Your integrity is your testimony.

Action: *Review one promise you have delayed and take a concrete step this week to fulfill it.*

Let us pray

1. *Father, forgive me for every unkept promise, in Jesus' name.*
2. *Lord, make me faithful in little and much, in Jesus' name.*
3. *Holy Spirit, give me courage to honor my vows fully, in Jesus' name.*
4. *Father, help me reflect Your faithfulness daily, in Jesus' name.*
5. *Lord, bless my obedience and open new doors as I keep my word, in Jesus' name.*

Prophetic Prayer of the Week

1. ***"Instead of shame you shall have double honor." (Isaiah 61:7).*** *Every shame in my life is replaced with honor and restoration, in Jesus' name.*
2. ***"You have found favor with God." (Luke 1:30).*** *The favor of God surrounds my life and opens doors everywhere I go, in Jesus' name.*
3. ***"God has not given us a spirit of fear." (2 Timothy 1:7).*** *My mind is restored to peace, power, and soundness, in Jesus' name.*

Tuesday 16 June

HOW TO FORGIVE FROM THE HEART

Read: Matthew 18:21-35

Bible in 1 year: Exo. 21-24
Bible in 2 years: Luke 17

"This is how my heavenly Father will treat each of you unless you forgive your brother or sister from your heart" (Matthew 18:35).

Forgiveness is not complete until it comes from the heart. The Greek word for heart, *kardia*, refers to the inner self—the mind, emotions, and will. To forgive from the heart means more than saying polite words; it is a deep release of resentment and a surrender to God's grace.

Jesus gave this command after the parable of the unforgiving servant. That servant was forgiven a great debt yet refused to forgive a small one. His story reminds us that forgiveness is not optional; it is the natural response of a heart transformed by God's mercy.

But how do we forgive from the heart? First, acknowledge the hurt honestly. Denial keeps wounds buried, but Christ heals what we bring into the light. Second, pray for the offender. As difficult as it feels, prayer softens our hearts and shifts our focus from pain to God's power. Third, release the debt to God. Forgiveness does not mean excusing sin—it means handing over the right to revenge. Fourth, choose forgiveness daily. Feelings may linger, but forgiveness is a decision you reaffirm until healing comes.

Action: *Have you told someone that you have forgiven them, but your heart is bitter against them? Go before God and prayerfully apply the* *four steps above.*

Let us pray

1. *Father, thank You for forgiving me completely through Christ, in Jesus' name.*
2. *Lord, help me forgive every offense from the depth of my heart, in Jesus' name.*
3. *Father, heal my emotions and release me from hidden resentment, in Jesus' name.*
4. *Lord, give me grace to pray for those who have hurt me, in Jesus' name.*
5. *Father, let forgiveness flow through me as a testimony of Your mercy, in Jesus' name.*

Wednesday 17 June

FORGIVING DOES NOT MEAN FORGETTING

Read: Isaiah 43:25

Bible in 1 year: Exo. 25-27
Bible in 2 years: Luke 18

"I, even I, am he who blots out your transgressions, for my own sake, and remembers your sins no more" (Isaiah 43:25 NIV).

Many people struggle with forgiveness because they confuse it with forgetting. They think, *"If I forgive, I must erase the memory."* But true forgiveness does not require forgetting—it requires releasing. The Hebrew word for "remember" in Isaiah 43:25, *zakar*, does not mean God has no memory of sin. It means He chooses not to call it to account. Forgiveness is not the erasing of memory but the canceling of a debt.

God does not expect us to wipe our memories clean. Painful events may linger in our minds for years. What He asks is that when those memories surface, we choose not to dwell on them in bitterness or use them as weapons against others. Forgiveness means refusing to let the offense control our present and future.

A testimony of Corrie ten Boom illustrates this truth. After surviving a Nazi concentration camp, she met one of the guards who had abused prisoners. He asked for her forgiveness. Corrie admitted she could not forget the cruelty, but by God's grace, she forgave him. She later said, *"Forgiveness is an act of the will, and the will can function regardless of the temperature of the heart."* Choosing to forgive doesn't mean the offense wasn't serious or that trust is immediately restored. It means you no longer hold on to revenge or resentment. Forgetting may be impossible, but forgiving is always possible through Christ.

Action: *Is there someone who has hurt you? Go before God, forgive, and ask for healing in your heart.*

Let us pray

1. *Father, thank You for forgiving me and not holding my sins against me, in Jesus' name.*
2. *Lord, help me release every offense, even if I still remember the pain, in Jesus' name.*
3. *Father, heal my heart from every wound caused by past offenses, in Jesus' name.*
4. *Lord, give me the grace to forgive even when memories remain, in Jesus' name.*
5. *Father, let my forgiveness be a testimony of Your love and mercy, in Jesus' name.*

Thursday 18 June

FORGIVENESS HEALS FAMILIES

Read: Colossians 3:13

Bible in 1 year: Exo. 28-31
Bible in 2 years: Luke 19

"Bear with each other and forgive one another if any of you has a grievance against someone. Forgive as the Lord forgave you"(Colossians 3:13 NIV).

Family wounds often cut the deepest. The Greek word for forgive, *charizomai*, means to show grace or freely pardon. Within families, forgiveness is essential for healing generational hurts, misunderstandings, and broken trust. Without forgiveness, small conflicts grow into years of silence, division, and bitterness.

The Bible gives us a powerful example in the story of Jacob and Esau. After years of deception and betrayal, Esau had every reason to hate his brother. Yet when they met again, instead of revenge, Esau embraced Jacob with tears of reconciliation (Genesis 33:4). Forgiveness healed a broken family and restored peace.

In many homes today, unforgiveness destroys marriages, divides siblings, and alienates parents from children. The enemy thrives in such division because where there is strife, there is no peace. But forgiveness shuts the door to the enemy and invites God's healing presence.

I once heard of a father and son who hadn't spoken for ten years because of a misunderstanding. After hearing a sermon on forgiveness, the father made the first move. He wrote a letter asking forgiveness, and that simple step melted years of bitterness.

When forgiveness enters a family, walls fall down, trust begins to rebuild, and love flows again. Families thrive not because they are perfect, but because they practice forgiveness daily.

Action: *Spend time this week seeking God's wisdom on how to deal with the unforgiveness in your family.*

Let us pray

1. *Father, thank You for forgiving my family and me through Christ, in Jesus' name.*
2. *Lord, heal every broken relationship in my family, in Jesus' name.*
3. *Father, give me the humility and courage to forgive my family members, in Jesus' name.*
4. *Lord, let forgiveness restore love and unity in my home, in Jesus' name.*
5. *Father, make my family a testimony of reconciliation and healing, in Jesus' name.*

Read: Revelation 3:14–22

Bible in 1 year: Exo. 32-34
Bible in 2 years: Luke 20

"And even if our gospel is veiled, it is veiled to those who are perishing. The god of this age has blinded the minds of unbelievers, so that they cannot see the light of the gospel that displays the glory of Christ, who is the image of God." (2 Corinthians 4:3–4 NIV)

Spiritual blindness is the most dangerous condition a human being can suffer. Physical blindness limits your movement, but spiritual blindness limits your destiny. It keeps you from knowing the living and merciful God. It disconnects you from the path God prepared for your life. It gives you a distorted image of who you are and casts a dark veil over your mind, preventing you from seeing the glory of Christ revealed through the Gospel.

The church in Laodicea is a sober example of what happens when spiritual blindness enters the life of believers. Outwardly, they were rich, influential, and proud of their success. They lived in a prosperous city known for banking, textile wealth, and eye medicine—yet Jesus said they were wretched, miserable, poor, blind, and naked. Their blindness made them think they were spiritually strong, while in reality, they were far from the true light. They could not see their desperate need for Christ. They could not recognize their lukewarmness. They could not discern their spiritual poverty. Pride had made them blind.

This is the danger for many today. Pride blinds.

Prejudice blinds. The pursuit of power blinds. Even the opinions of people can blind us, preventing us from seeing the glorious riches Christ has made available to us. The enemy works tirelessly to cloud our minds so we cannot see clearly the beauty, truth, and transforming power of the Gospel.

We need our eyes healed. We must see ourselves in the light of the Gospel—with humility, simplicity, purity, and obedience. Christ calls us to buy "eye salve" from Him, meaning we must allow the Holy Spirit to open our understanding, soften our hearts, and remove every veil from our minds.

And we must preach the Gospel boldly. We cannot overcome this age's blindness unless we shine the light. The more we see Christ, the more clearly we can show Him to others.

Action: *Pray for the Holy Spirit to remove every veil from your mind and open your eyes to see Christ, yourself, and others clearly.*

Let us pray

1. *Father, thank You for sending Jesus, the true Light who opens the eyes of the blind, in Jesus' name.*
2. *Lord, heal every area of my life where spiritual blindness has limited my growth, in Jesus' name.*
3. *Father, deliver me from pride, prejudice, and every influence that blinds my spiritual vision, in Jesus' name.*
4. *Lord, give me clear sight to understand Your Word, obey Your voice, and walk in Your truth daily, in Jesus' name.*
5. *I decree that every veil over my life is torn, and I shall walk in the light of Christ with clarity and power, in Jesus' name.*

Saturday 20 June

THE POWER OF SHARED BURDENS

Read: James 5:13–20

Bible in 1 year: Exo. 35-37
Bible in 2 years: Luke 21

"Confess your trespasses to one another, and pray for one another, that you may be healed. The effective, fervent prayer of a righteous man avails much." (James 5:16)

The church is often mistakenly viewed as a collection of isolated individuals who happen to worship in the same place. In reality, it is a living, breathing family—a body bound together by the Spirit of God. James 5:16 highlights a vital aspect of this family life: the power of bearing one another's burdens through intercessory prayer. When we confess our struggles and lift them up in prayer together, we create a channel for divine healing and restoration. The "effective, fervent prayer" mentioned by James is not a casual wish; it is an intense, purposeful alignment of our hearts with God's will, which releases His power into the lives of others.

The early church understood that they were better together. In Acts 12:5–7, when Peter was imprisoned and facing certain death, the church did not just send him a letter of encouragement; they prayed "earnestly" for him. That collective, fervent prayer moved heaven, and God dispatched an angel to open the prison doors. This is the blueprint for our intercession today. When we choose to stand in the gap for someone else, we are not just helping them; we are inviting divine intervention into their impossible situation. Our shared burdens act as a bridge for God's miraculous power to cross over into the lives of the hurting.

Who are you praying for today? It is easy to become so consumed with our own battles that we forget the responsibility we have to our brothers and sisters. If you are struggling, don't suffer in silence—find a godly friend and share your burden. If you are strong, look for someone who is weary and offer to stand with them in prayer. We were never designed to carry the weight of our challenges alone. Today, make a commitment to be an intercessor. When the body of Christ prays in unity, there is no barrier that can remain locked and no wound that cannot be touched by His healing power.

Action: *Choose one person today to intercede for intentionally; call or message them to let them know you are lifting their specific burden before God.*

Let us pray

1) *Lord, teach me to be a faithful burden-bearer for those in my church family.*
2) *Heal those who are hurting, broken, or discouraged in our midst, Lord.*
3) *Strengthen our church in true unity and sacrificial love.*
4) *Let our fervent, corporate prayer release Your power in our community.*
5) *Make me an intercessor who stands in the gap for the needs of others daily.*

Sunday 21 June

FROM TEARS INTO TRIUMPH

Read: Psalm 126:1–6

Bible in 1 year: Exo. 38-40
Bible in 2 years: Luke 22

"He who goes out weeping, carrying seed to sow, will return with songs of joy, carrying sheaves with him." (Psalm 126:6)

Psalm 126 is a song of restoration, celebrating how the Lord brought Israel back from captivity until their mouths were filled with laughter. However, it also reveals a profound spiritual law: the most significant harvests often begin with sowing in tears. The emphasis here is not on the sower's skill or talent, but on their faithfulness to keep showing up even when the ground is hard. The Hebrew word for "goes out" (*halak*) implies a continual, intentional movement. It suggests that God values the time you invest in His presence—even when that time feels costly or painful—far more than any outward display of ability.

Your greatest offering to God is not your ability, but your availability. We often measure our worth by what we can "do" for the Kingdom, yet God is looking for the "intentional movement" of a heart that refuses to stop seeking Him. Every minute spent in prayer and every tear shed in worship is a seed planted in eternity. God specializes in turning time spent with Him in our moments of weakness into a supernatural harvest of joy.

Consider the biblical example of Hannah. She had no impressive title or public platform; she simply gave God her time in persistent, tearful prayer at the temple. She poured out her soul in a season of deep distress, and God saw those tears as seeds. He transformed her private weeping into a public testimony of triumph when her son, Samuel, was born. Are you the kind of believer who stops sowing because the season is difficult? Remember that your tears in prayer are never wasted; they are the very investments that produce your future songs of joy. Tears are seeds for recovery!

Prophetic Declaration: *I declare that my tears are seeds, my time with God is treasure, and my harvest shall be joy! As I give Him my time, He will turn my mourning into dancing!*

Let us pray

1. *Father, teach me to value my quiet time with You more than any public talent.*
2. *Lord, give me the grace to sow faithfully in prayer, even when it feels like I am sowing through tears.*
3. *O Lord, let my joy be rooted in Your presence rather than my own performance.*
4. *Holy Spirit, transform my current seasons of weeping into a testimony of laughter.*
5. *Father, make my entire life a continual offering of time spent at Your feet.*

Monday 22 June

WHY YOU BECOME DISCOURAGED

Read: Numbers 21:4-5

Bible in 1 year: Jam. 1-2
Bible in 2 years: Luke 23

"Therefore, we do not lose heart. Though outwardly we are wasting away, yet inwardly we are being renewed day by day" (2 Corinthians 4:16).

Discouragement doesn't mean you lack faith; it means you are human. Even as a believer, your heart can grow heavy when pressure lasts longer than expected. Israel's *"Soul became discouraged on the way"* because the journey felt endless. You experience the same thing when hardship fills your vision. Bills pile up, prayers seem unanswered, strength feels low, and before long, your focus shifts from who God is to how hard life feels. When you stare too long at the difficulty, your hope begins to fade.

Another reason you become discouraged is comparison. You look at others and wonder why their prayers seem to be answered faster, their progress seems smoother, their calling appears clearer, or they are supposedly more blessed than you. Comparison quietly tells you that you are behind or failing. But God never asked you to run someone else's race. Like Elijah, you can feel isolated and defeated, even after moments of victory, simply because you forget that you are not alone and that God is still working beyond what you see.

You also become discouraged when you forget what God has already done. Psalm 103:2 urges you not to forget His benefits, because forgetting weakens your courage.

Discouragement often comes from spiritual amnesia – forgetfulness. The word "discourage" carries the idea of being shattered inwardly or losing heart – weariness that drains courage from the inside out. When past deliverances fade from memory, today's challenges feel heavier than they really are.

Think about a time God carried you through something you thought would break you. Today, you are still standing. That same God has not changed. What he did before, He will do again.

Action: *Today, deliberately remember, refocus, and trust God with what lies in front of you.*

Let us pray

1. *Father, thank You for Your past faithfulness and every victory You have given me.*
2. *O Lord, help me to focus on You instead of my hardships, in Jesus' name.*
3. *Free my heart from comparison and help me run my own race, in Jesus' name.*
4. *Father, remind me daily of what You have already done for me, in Jesus' name.*
5. *I command every voice of anxiety in my soul to be silenced by the blood of Jesus, in Jesus' name.*

Prophetic Prayer of the Week

1. ***"Those who sow in tears shall reap in joy." (Psalm 126:5).*** *I will not miss my harvest this season, in Jesus' name.*
2. **"Even the demons are subject to us in Your name." (Luke 10:17).** *My spiritual authority increases and every demonic force flees, in Jesus' name.*

3. ***"I will restore to you the years." (Joel 2:25).*** *Every wasted season of my life is redeemed by God's power, in Jesus' name.*

Tuesday 23 June

THE PERIL OF THE HALF-HEARTED

Read: Jeremiah 29:11-14;
Revelation 3:15-16

Bible in 1 year: Jam. 3-5
Bible in 2 years: Luke 24

"And you will seek Me and find Me, when you search for Me with all your heart." (Jeremiah 29:13)

The promise of finding God is not given to the casual observer, but to the diligent seeker. In Jeremiah's day, the Israelites were in exile, surrounded by the distractions of Babylon. God's message was clear: restoration begins with the heart. The Hebrew word for "search" in this passage implies a deep, intentional inquiry—like a man looking for hidden treasure. Many today complain that they cannot "feel" God or hear His voice, yet they only offer Him the leftovers of their day and the fringes of their focus.

Half-heartedness is a spiritual disease that creates a barrier between us and the manifest presence of God. In Revelation, Jesus warns the Laodicean church against being "lukewarm." A lukewarm heart wants the benefits of the Kingdom without the sacrifice of the King; it is a heart divided between worldly desires and the requirements of holiness. When we seek God with a divided heart, our spiritual frequency is jammed by competing interests. Biblical history shows that those who moved the hand of God—like Daniel or Elijah—were those who were "all in."

Ask yourself: Are you seeking God with your whole heart, or are you just "checking a box"? Are you the kind of believer who wonders why your spiritual life feels stagnant while you spend hours on entertainment and only minutes in the Word? Total surrender is the price of total discovery. Searching with "all your heart" involves a holy hunger that refuses to be satisfied with religious routine. When God sees a heart fully turned toward Him, He reveals Himself in ways that transform reality. Today, move from the crowd of the curious to the inner circle of the committed.

Prophetic Declaration: *I am a whole-hearted seeker! I refuse to be lukewarm! As I seek the Lord today, I shall surely find Him!*

Let us pray

1. *Father, forgive my divided heart and my distracted pursuit of You.*
2. *Lord, ignite a fire in my soul that cannot be quenched by worldly things.*
3. *Holy Spirit, expose every hidden idol competing for my attention today.*
4. *Lord, let my hunger for Your presence override every other appetite.*
5. *I receive the grace to move from a lukewarm routine into a red-hot pursuit!*

Wednesday 24 June

LOOKING UP IN FAITH

Read: Psalm 34:1–7

Bible in 1 year: Gal. 1-3
Bible in 2 years: Josh. 1-2

"I sought the Lord, and He answered me, and delivered me from all my fears." (Psalm 34:4)

Faith is never a passive state of mind; it is an active, intentional gaze toward the character of God. David's testimony in Psalm 34 reveals the transformative power of "seeking the Lord." Notice that David did not just seek a solution to his problem; he sought the Problem-Solver. When he looked up, God answered, and the result was total deliverance from his fears. To "look up" in faith means to deliberately shift our dependence from human systems, which are often fragile and prone to failure, toward the immutable throne of divine intervention. As Numbers 23:19 reminds us, "God is not a man, that He should lie; neither the son of man, that He should repent." His Word is the only solid ground for a weary soul.

Looking up to God yields two powerful outcomes. First, we receive divine light. His glory begins to radiate upon us, changing the internal landscape of our hearts even if our external circumstances remain challenging. Like Hannah at Shiloh, who poured out her heart despite the mockery of her rival, looking up turns our "Shiloh" moment into a place of divine encounter. Second, when we look to Him, we are never put to shame. Trusting God is a risk that always pays off because His promises are "Yes and Amen" (2 Corinthians 1:20). When we prove our dependence on Him by putting aside every other "Plan B," He rises in our favor to defend our cause.

Do you have a "Plan B" that you are relying on more than God? Often, we claim to trust the Lord, but our actions reveal we are still clutching to human solutions just in case He fails. Looking up to God requires a total relinquishing of these alternatives. Today, decide that your gaze will not be downward at your limitations or outward at the world's chaos, but upward at His sufficiency. When you prove your absolute dependence on Him, you create the atmosphere for His power to manifest in your life.

Prophetic Declaration*:* *I declare that as I look up to God in faith, His light shines upon me, and I shall never be put to shame! My trust is in the Lord, and His faithfulness is my shield*

Let us Pray

1. *Lord, teach me to look up to You in faith, especially when my circumstances are overwhelming.*
2. *Let Your light radiate upon my life and clear the fog of my confusion.*
3. *Deliver me from the grip of fear and the paralyzing weight of shame.*
4. *Help me to lay aside all my secondary, human options and rely on You alone.*
5. *Lord, fulfill the specific promises You have spoken over my life.!*

Thursday 25 June **RADIANT FACES OF FAITH**

Read: Exodus 34:29–35

Bible in 1 year: Gal. 4-6
Bible in 2 years: Josh. 3-4

"Now it was so, when Moses came down from Mount Sinai (and the two tablets of the Testimony were in Moses' hand when he came down from the mountain), that Moses did not know that the skin of his face shone while he talked with Him." (Exodus 34:29)

The Hebrew word *nahar*—meaning to shine, beam, or radiate with joy—captures the visible transformation of those who spend significant time in the presence of the Almighty. When Moses descended from the mountain, he was unaware that his face was emitting a heavenly glow; he had been so completely immersed in the glory of God that the encounter left a physical mark upon him. This radiance is never self-made. It is not the result of human effort, personality, or a well-rehearsed demeanor. It is the authentic, undeniable reflection of God's own light shining through the life of a believer. When we look up in faith and linger in His presence, we are inherently changed.

This radiance acts as a spiritual signal to the world. Just as Moses had to put a veil over his face because the people could not bear the brightness, those who dwell in the secret place of the Most High carry a "glory" that others can sense, even if they cannot explain it. It is a peace that passes understanding and a joy that defies temporary setbacks. When the glory of God rests upon us, despair naturally gives way to hope, and fear is replaced by a godly courage. This is the hallmark of the radiant believer: a countenance that reflects not the darkness of the world's circumstances, but the brilliance of the King's presence.

Are you living in a way that others can tell you have been with Jesus? Often, we are so occupied with the "veil" of our daily responsibilities that we fail to spend enough time in the light to let it change us. True radiance is not a mask; it is a byproduct of deep, unhurried prayer and worship. Today, determine to spend time in His presence until His light begins to mark your life. Let His peace settle your heart and His joy brighten your perspective. When you carry the radiance of God, you become a living invitation for others to seek the same Source of light.

Action: *Spend time today in intentional worship and silent prayer, asking God to illuminate your countenance with His glory as you dwell in His presence.*

Let us pray

1. *Lord, let the glory of Your presence shine upon my life in an undeniable way.*
2. *Make me radiant with Your peace, so that others see Your beauty in me.*
3. *Deliver me from the darkness of hidden fears and anxieties that dim my light.*
4. *Fill me with a joy that is so deep it overflows to everyone I encounter.*
5. *Let my life and my testimony draw the lost to You, the true Light.*

Friday 26 June

GROWING DEEPER IN WORSHIP

Read: 2 Peter 1:1–8

Bible in 1 year: Isa. 1-3
Bible in 2 years: Josh. 5-6

"For this very reason, make every effort to add to your faith goodness; and to goodness, knowledge; and to knowledge, self-control; and to self-control, perseverance; and to perseverance, godliness." (2 Peter 1:5–6)

Spiritual growth is not a passive process; it is a dedicated commitment to becoming more like Christ. Many believers mistakenly think that worship is reserved for Sunday mornings or specific musical sets, but Peter reveals that worship is fundamentally about character transformation. He reminds us that God has already provided everything we need for life and godliness through His divine power. Our responsibility is to "make every effort" to add specific virtues to our faith, such as goodness, knowledge, and self-control. True worship is the lifestyle that emerges when we cooperate with the Holy Spirit to cultivate these graces within us.

Worship that does not lead to change is merely a performance. To grow deeper, we must move beyond the superficial aspects of religious activity and confront the areas of our lives that are still governed by "dangerous contentment." Complacency is the greatest enemy of worship. When we stop desiring more of God, we stop growing. The early believers in Acts 2:42 were characterized by their devotion to the Word, prayer, and fellowship—they understood that their worship was not an event but a lifestyle. Their devotion was the nutrient that sustained their growth, and it should be the same for us today.

Are you settling for a stagnant spiritual life, or are you actively pursuing the "more" that God has promised? Growth in worship means that we are constantly yielding our old, sinful patterns to the Spirit and inviting His character to replace them. It is a lifelong process, nourished by consistent time in the Word and a willingness to be refined by the Father. Today, identify one area—whether it is patience, love, or obedience—where you have felt stagnant. Intentionally surrender that area to God, and ask Him to use it as a catalyst for deeper worship in your life.

Action: *Identify one area of your character where you know you need growth and spend ten minutes in prayer today, specifically asking for the Holy Spirit to refine that area.*

Let us pray

1. *Lord, help me to commit fully to spiritual growth, rejecting any form of complacency.*
2. *Teach me to actively add goodness, knowledge, and love to my faith, day by day.*
3. *Deliver me from the trap of dangerous contentment, and ignite a fresh hunger for You.*
4. *Nourish me daily with Your Word and Spirit so that I may mature in my walk.*
5. *Make my worship a reflection of Christ's nature, not just a song I sing.*

Saturday 27 June

TRANSFORMATIONAL WORSHIP

Read: Colossians 3:12–17

Bible in 1 year: Isa. 4-6
Bible in 2 years: Josh. 7-8

"Let the word of Christ dwell in you richly in all wisdom, teaching and admonishing one another in psalms and hymns and spiritual songs, singing with grace in your hearts to the Lord." (Colossians 3:16)

Worship is the intersection of divine truth and human expression. Paul instructs the Colossians to let the "word of Christ dwell in you richly," indicating that our worship is only as deep as the reservoir of Scripture within us. Music is a beautiful, powerful connector, but true worship grows deeper when it is anchored in truth, prayer, and a heart overflowing with thanksgiving. When the Word saturates our minds, our songs of praise shift from being emotional reactions to being profound declarations of who God is. This is how worship transforms both the worshiper and the environment.

Obstacles such as comfort, a refusal to self-evaluate, or a lack of spiritual discipline can quickly stunt our growth. Paul and Silas in Acts 16:25 serve as our greatest example of transformative worship. Imprisoned, beaten, and bound in the deepest part of a dungeon, they did not wait for their circumstances to change before they began to worship. They chose to worship *in* the middle of their crisis. God responded with a supernatural earthquake that broke their chains and opened the prison doors. This demonstrates that worship is not about where we are; it is about who we are looking at.

Is your worship conditioned by your circumstances? If you only praise God when things are going well, you have yet to discover the power of transformative worship. Today, stop evaluating your life through the lens of your current problems and start evaluating it through the lens of God's Word. When you worship from a heart that is rooted in Scripture, you are not merely singing; you are changing the atmosphere around you. You are inviting the power of God to manifest in your life, regardless of how dark the "prison" might seem.

Prophetic Declaration: *I declare that my worship is growing deeper, rooted in the Word, overflowing with thanksgiving, and transforming my life! I will not worship from a place of arrival, but from a heart that longs for more of God!*

Let us pray

1. *Lord, let Your Word dwell richly in me, fueling my worship with truth and depth.*
2. *Fill my heart with such profound gratitude that praise becomes my natural language.*
3. *Help me to overcome every obstacle to my spiritual growth, especially complacency.*
4. *Teach me to worship You in spirit and in truth, not just with my lips, but with my life.*
5. *Let my worship bring the transformation of Your Kingdom into my life and community.*

Sunday 28 June

MIRACLES IN OUR MIDST

Read: Acts 19:8–12

Bible in 1 year: Isa. 7-9
Bible in 2 years: Josh. 9; 10:1-20

"Now God worked unusual miracles by the hands of Paul, so that even handkerchiefs or aprons that had touched him were taken to the sick, and their illnesses were cured and the evil spirits left them." (Acts 19:11–12)

God is still in the business of performing miracles. His supernatural power is not a relic reserved for the pages of history; it is the living evidence of His presence today. The account in Acts 19 of God working "unusual miracles" through Paul reveals that when a believer is fully surrendered and saturated with the presence of God, the supernatural becomes a natural occurrence. Miracles serve as signs that point to the reality of the Kingdom. They bring restoration where there was ruin, favor where there was rejection, and breakthrough where there was a stalemate. Miracles remind us that God is not limited by the laws of science or the finality of human impossibility.

When the church prays, heaven responds. The frequency of miracles in our lives is often linked to the depth of our expectancy. Do you believe that God is the same yesterday, today, and forever? When we approach God with a heart of worship and a spirit of faith, He delights in releasing His power to glorify His name. A miracle is not just a solution to a problem; it is a demonstration of God's sovereignty. It proves that He is Lord over every sickness, every storm, and every darkness that attempts to hold His people captive.

Are you allowing your circumstances to dictate your view of God's power? Perhaps you have faced disappointment and have started to settle for a "natural" life, believing that God no longer moves in big ways. Today, challenge that mindset. Start praying for the supernatural to break into your day-to-day existence. Whether it is healing in your body, a breakthrough in your finances, or restoration in a fractured relationship, God is eager to display His power. Step out in faith, stop limiting the Holy One of Israel, and watch as He manifests His glory in your midst.

Prophetic Declaration*: I declare that miracles are released in my life, my family, and my church today! Restoration, favor, and breakthroughs manifest in Jesus' name!*

Let us pray

1. *Lord, release Your miraculous power into my life, my family, and our church.*
2. *Restore everything that has been broken by the enemy in our lives, Lord.*
3. *Grant me the breakthrough and favor I need in this season, for Your glory.*
4. *Let the supernatural be a common, daily experience in my walk with You.*
5. *Glorify Your name, Lord, through signs and wonders that draw others to the truth.*

Monday 29 June

THE CLARITY OF DIVINE GUIDANCE

Read: Proverbs 3:5–10

Bible in 1 year: Isa. 10-12
Bible in 2 years: Josh. 10:21-43; 11

"Trust in the Lord with all your heart, and lean not on your own understanding; in all your ways acknowledge Him, and He shall direct your paths." (Proverbs 3:5–6)

Clarity is the currency of the Kingdom. In a season of enlargement and breakthrough, we are often tempted to move faster than God, relying on our "own understanding" to map out the future. However, Proverbs 3:5–6 provides a foundational principle for the advancing believer: total trust. When we rely on our own intellect, we are limited by our past experiences and our finite perspectives. When we acknowledge Him in all our ways, we tap into the infinite wisdom of the One who sees the end from the beginning. Divine guidance is not just about avoiding mistakes; it is about hitting the targets that God has ordained for your life.

The promise here is clear: *He shall direct your paths.* This means that God is actively involved in the logistics of your journey. He is not a silent spectator; He is a guiding Shepherd. Many of the frustrations we experience in our careers, our ministries, or our relationships are the direct result of moving forward without His explicit direction. By acknowledging Him—bringing Him into the decision-making process before we act—we surrender our right to be "right" and open the door for His perfect strategy. This humble posture is the prerequisite for divine speed and accurate expansion.

How do you make your major decisions? Do you pray *after* you have already decided, or do you seek His wisdom *before* you form a plan? Acknowledging God means making Him your primary consultant. When you trust Him with all your heart, you are relieved of the burden of needing to figure everything out. Today, stop trying to over-analyze your situation. Bring your choices before the Lord, ask for His perspective, and be willing to change your direction if He nudges you. When you align your path with His, you will find that doors open with less resistance and you reach your destination with greater clarity.

Prophetic Declaration: *I declare that my steps are ordered by the Lord! I do not lean on my own understanding; I trust Him completely, and He leads me into the success He has prepared for me!*

Let us pray

1. *Lord, I surrender my understanding and rely entirely on Your wisdom.*
2. *Help me to acknowledge You in every decision, big or small, today.*
3. *Direct my paths, Lord, and close every door that is not part of Your perfect plan.*
4. *Deliver me from the pride of thinking I can handle this season without You.*
5. *Give me a heart that is sensitive to Your guidance, whether it comes through a whisper or Your Word.*

Prophetic Prayer of the Week

1. ***"Write the vision and make it plain." (Habakkuk 2:2).*** *My vision is clear and I walk confidently in God's direction, in Jesus' name.*

2. ***"My horn you have exalted like a wild ox; I have been anointed with fresh oil." (Psalm 92:10).*** *Fresh oil and strength will rest upon my life daily, in Jesus' name.*
3. ***"You shall spread out to the right and to the left." (Isaiah 54:3).*** *My life expands into divine enlargement and increase, in Jesus' name.*

Tuesday 30 June **DIVINE REST**

Read: Exodus 33:12–16

Bible in 1 year: Isa. 13-15
Bible in 2 years: (Catch-up)

"And He said, 'My Presence will go with you, and I will give you rest.'" (Exodus 33:14)

In the midst of the wilderness, when the burden of leading a nation felt insurmountable, Moses sought a promise that went beyond mere logistical victory. He asked for the assurance of God's Presence. The Lord's reply—that His Presence would go with Moses to provide "rest"—is a profound revelation regarding how we should approach our assignments. True rest is not the cessation of activity; it is the assurance of divine partnership. It is the peace that comes from knowing that the One who called you is the One who will walk with you through every step of the expansion. Without His Presence, the effort to "enlarge" our borders is nothing more than a tiring pursuit of human ambition.

The rest God offers is a spiritual fortress. It allows us to work with vigor and passion, yet remain untroubled by the storms that inevitably arise when we are advancing into new territories. When we are walking in divine rest, we are not driven by the fear of failure or the pressure to perform; we are led by the assurance of His guidance. Think of the peace that sustained Jesus in the boat during the storm. He was able to rest because He knew His Father's purpose was greater than the waves. This is the quality of rest that is available to every believer who prioritizes the Presence above the project.

Are you exhausted by the "weight" of your current responsibilities? Perhaps you are working hard but missing the mark because you have left the Presence behind. Today, pause and realign. Stop asking for more resources, more time, or more recognition, and start asking for a greater awareness of His Presence. When God goes with you, your labor becomes light and your strategy becomes supernatural. Divine rest will sharpen your focus, renew your strength, and ensure that your expansion is sustainable. You are not meant to carry the weight of your destiny alone; you are meant to carry it in the comfort of His company.

Action: *Today, start every task with a simple prayer: "Lord, I am not doing this alone; come with me." Observe how your peace levels change as you maintain this awareness.*

Let us pray

1. *Lord, I value Your Presence above every task or goal I have for this season.*
2. *Grant me Your divine rest, so that I may work without the burden of anxiety.*
3. *Teach me to walk in step with Your Spirit, knowing You are guiding my every move.*
4. *Deliver me from the trap of working in my own strength, Lord.*
5. *May my labor be a reflection of my rest in You, producing fruit that lasts.*

WHAT YOUR SUPPORT WILL DO

It is very clear through the numerous miracles, breakthroughs and transformation of lives that God has chosen to use this ministry to stir a revival among His people in Cameroon and beyond. I received the call alone but I cannot execute it alone. You have a unique role to play in this divine project. Join us as we take the Gospel to every corner of Cameroon and beyond.

We want to start placing copies of this book in hotels, hospitals, schools and homes, to touch the lives of people with the gospel of Jesus Christ. Just as you have been blessed by this book, they too will be mightily blessed.

TESTIMONY

Every month, hundreds of copies of this Prayer Storm Daily Prayer Guide are distributed freely, thanks to the kind gesture of our partners. May God bless all of you who faithfully sponsor this outreach through your financial seed. You too can sponsor 10, 25, 50, 100 or even more copies to be printed and distributed charge-free to those who are hungry for the word.

Call the numbers: (237) 699.90.26.18 or 674.49.58.95 send an email to voiceofrevivalcameroon@yahoo.com.

If you want to become a distributor of our literature, contact us directly and we will give you the directives on how to do so.

WHERE TO BUY THIS PRAYER GUIDE

<u>CRN Centres</u>

- **Yaounde:** ***Prayer Storm Headquarters:*** 1st Floor Storey Building at Entrée Lycée de Tsinga village on the edge of the main road. **Contact:** 681.72.24.04/ 696.56.58.64
- **Bamenda:** Revival Christian Book Center, **Cow Street**: 675.14.04.50/ 694.20.04.51
- **Douala/PK 8:** All American Depot opposite Lycée **Cité des Palmiers**: 678.04.11.41/ 696.90.76.09/ 670.34.42.32

<u>Adamawa</u>

- **Banyo:** FGM: 677.92.05.98/ 674.64.71.31
- **Meinganga:** EEL: 699.65.02.67/ 652.70.40.68
- **Ngaoundere:** EEC Mont des Oliviers: 674.14.20.51, EEL: 690.06.37.14
- **Tibati:** EEC: 681.01.33.34

<u>Centre</u>

- **Eseka:** FGM: 675.07.56.24
- **Mbalmayo:** EEC: 675.12.86.85/
- **Mfou:** FGM: 677.36.43.28
- **Monatelé:** FGM: 677.58.42.99
- **Yaounde:** EEC **Biyem-assi**: 675.61.86.00/ 677.49.95.83/ 691.26.18.08, EEC **Nlongkak**: 677.56.41.09, EEC **Nouvelle Alliance**: 670.80.56.93, FGM **Biyem-assi**: 675.14.72.70, FGM **Etoug-Ebé**: 671.47.75.78/ 673.50.42.33, Galaxy Computers, Châteaux **Ngoa-Ekelle**: 670.52.75.26, **Yaounde: Librairie Chrétienne** Les Champions op. Total Caveau, **Mvog-Ada**: 675.51.02.86, **LC Maison de la Grâce**, Montée Jouvence op. Olympia: 675.38.46.96, **LC Maison de la**

Bénédiction, Marché Nsam: 691.64.47.84, **LC la Rhema**, Marché Essos, Terminus: 679.39.37.42, **LC Maison du Salut**, Pharmacie du Soleil, Carrefour MEEC: 674.85.16.33/ 699.33.85.11, **LC Livre de Vie**, Mini ferme: 675.00.45.60, **LC Bethesda**, Tsinga: 679.97.06.26, **Overcomers Christian Bookshop**, op. Djongolo Hospital, EtoaMeki: 677.16.46.20, **Mount Zion Christian Bookshop**, op. SONEL TKC: 663.25.86.23 / 675.21.94.35, **Tongolo**: 675.62.86.00, **Olembe**: 651.63.52.34, **DGI-Carrefour Abbia** 652.22.22.49, **Messassi**: 675.24.70.73, **Nkozoa**: 670.29.50.18, **Essos**: 677.53.94.52, **Odzja**: 679.97.47.08, **Etoug-Ebé**: 675.37.18.11, **Mimboman**: 699.90.52.84, **Poste Centrale**: 650.70.08.07, **Emombo**: 699.90.52.84, **Lycée Emana**: 677.86.23.14

East

- **Batouri:** FGM: 664.86.41.80
- **Bertoua:** CBC, **quartier Ngaikada** ou **Aprilé centrale** sous-préfecture: 678.00.63.20/ 694.25.69.20, Collège Bilingue de l'Orient, entrée Hôpital Régionale, **quartier Italy**: 670.56.81.49, FGM, **Nkolbikon**: 696.57.95.43, 677.65.46.76, FGM, **Tigaza**: 674.15.13.18
- **Yokadouma:** FGM: 673.16.24.95/ 696.51.73.70

Far-North

- **Maroua:** Église Missionnaire du Réveil (EMIR) **Baoliwop**: 694.43.33.63, FGM **Harde**: 675.33.12.27, Roman Catholic Church: 673.15.19.76
- **Yagoua:** FGM: 675.691.869

Littoral

Douala: Dakar: La Gloire Phone, immeuble X Tigi, Commissariat 11e: 697.60.57.85, **Kotto:** Behind Neptune fuel station, **Bloc M:** 677.68.18.52, **Bonaberi:** 677.89.87.46, **Akwa:** 691.04.14.59/ 677.91.29.45, **Logpom:** 677.68.18.52/ 651.78.57.30**,** **Carrefour Lycée de Maképé:** 698.09.42.63, **PK 12 (Marché):** 677.91.29.45/ 696.13.99.26, **Texaco-Nkoulouluon:** 675.18.79.85/695112610 691.04.14.59, **Terminus Saint Michel :** 675187985, La Gloire Phone, Maison X. Tigi, **Carrefour entrée Bille:** 678.19.90.85, **PK 21:** 670.79.05.40/ 691.04.14.59, **Bonanjo:** 691.04.14.59, 677061705 691.04.14.59, **Ange Raphael ESSEC:** 694.26.12.28/ 677.91.29.45, 698360441, **Bonamoussadi Maetur:** 694.26.12.28/ 677.91.29.45, **Village:** 670.79.05.40/ 691.04.14.5, Sure Foundation **Bonabéri:** Ancienne route op. Lycée de Bonaberi Winners Chapel: 671.403.761

- **Nkongsamba:** FGM: 676.40.90.55
- **Melong - GCEPAL:** Tel: 677.80.16.45

North

- **Garoua:** FGM: 678.67.04.22/ 699.91.91.65

North-West

- **Bamenda:** Bamenda Main Market, **Shed 15**: 679.45.11.88, Carmel Cooperative Credit Union (CarCCUL), **Sonac Street**/Tél: 651.04.21.27, FGM NW1 Area office, opposite Garanti Express: 679.46.63.31, FGM, **Cow Street**: 677.21.97.22, FGM, **Mbomassa**: 683.40.40.88, Omega Fire Ministry, **Foncha junction**: 677.93.19.98, ACADI head office, **Wakiki junction**: 672.82.77.84, SUMAN Christian Book Center, **Sonac Street**: 675.72.91.32/ 665.49.98.48, Victory Computers, Food market, **Fishpond hill**: 677.64.19.54, Wailing Women: 696.00.35.07/ 674.57.36.76

- **Batibo:** FGM: 677.31.25.45
- **Njinikom/Mbingo:** BERUDA: 677.60.14.07
- **Jakiri:** FGM, **Nkar**: 677.73.82.91
- **Kumbo:** FGM: 675.72.91.32
- **Mbengwi:** FGM: 677.33.73.86
- **Ndop:** Bruno Bijouterie, Central park: 674.97.59.34
- **Wum:** FGM Central Town: 677.64.32.56, PCC Kesu: 677.13.83.51

West

- **Bafang:** FGM, **Bafang**: 655.00.25.57
- **Bafia:** FGM: 675.21.92.95/ 695.54.96.14
- **Bafoussam:** Alliance biblique du Cameroun, **Tamdja**, SOREPCO: 699.74.79.10, Radio Bonne Nouvelle: 699.93.09.32, Librairie chrétienne du **Camp** oignon: 699.51.47.25, LC PAROLE DE VIE, **gare routière de** Ndiangdam: 699.75.50.99, Dépôt RAYON AMBIANCE **marché A**: 699.42.78.47, EEC **Tamdja**: 696.14.90.16, EEC **Kamkop**: 699.44.03.59, EEC **Plateau**: 696.17.54.23, EEC **Toket**: 695.56.43.61, EEC **SOCADA**: 697.85.65.65, EEC **Tyo-Baleng**: 670.89.70.52, EEC **Kouogouo**: 675.42.27.86, EEC **Diangdam**: 698.35.20.37, FGM **Kamkop**: 653.83.11.80, Faith Bible Church: 683.94.01.21
- **Baham:** FGM: 677.47.55.79
- **Bandjoun:** FGM: 676.41.49.09
- **Bangangte:** EEC **Banekane**: 677.86.47.68
- **Banyo:** FGM: 677.92.05.98/ 674.64.71.31
- **Dschang:** FGM: 675.18.79.85/ 656.20.07.02, FGM **Minmeto**: 681.08.78.37/ 655.01.81.09

- **Foumban:** Décoration Splendeur, **CAMOCO**/Tel.: 677.79.30.83/ 694.85.09.25
- **Kombou:** EEC: 675.81.36.07
- **Mbouda:** FGM: 696.10.41.33/ 676.36.18.11, Cyber Café Pressing near Espace Saint Pierre du Fossie, op. Party House: 675.00.91.15, EEC **Mbouda Centre**: 695.61.97.79

South

- **Ebolowa:** FGM: 677.66.00.19/ 671.90.97.22
- **Kribi:** Carrefour Django: 675.957.912
- **Kye-Ossi:** FGM: 678.78.00.90/ 699.95.96.99

South-West

- **Buea:** FGM **Molyko**: 677.86.47.68, Molyko, near Express Union, **Check Point**: 675.06.37.78,
- **Ekona:** FGM: 675.84.26.91
- **Kumba:** Caisse Populaire Coopérative Carmel (CarCCUL), **Sonac Street**: 675.45.12.21, Glorious Christian Book Center, **Sonac Street**: 677.62.58.49
- **Lebialem:** FGM de **Talung**, Bamumbu – Wabane: 670.466.121
- **Limbe:** Librairie Amen, **New town**: 677.16.51.62, FGM **Mawoh**: 675.78.94.19, FGM **Cow Fence**: 675.73.20.02
- **Misaje:** Kingdom Restoration Parish (KRP) **opposite the hospital**: 679.33.66.53
- **Mutengene:** FGM: 675.36.36.84
- **Muyuka:** FGM: 673.428.985, Royal Priesthood Nursery and Primary School: 677.72.76.80
- **Tiko:** FGM: 654.88.75.57, 674.47.34.36
- **Tombel:** Baptist Church Waterfall: 677.92.33.58

ABROAD:

- **N'Djamena (Chad):** Evang. Kaltouma Aguidi: (235) 95.01.99.92
- **Libreville (Gabon):** Rev. Petipa Flaubert: (241) 05.31.27.39

Pay for your book orders (DISTRIBUTORS ONLY) at:
EcoBank, Acc. No: 0200212620638901 **or** ORANGE Mobile Money, Acc. No: 696880058
Info lines: (237) 677436964, 675686005, 673571953, 679465717;
crnprayerstorm@gmail.com,
prayerstorm@christianrestorationnetwork.org,
www.christianrestorationnetwork.org

Send Financial Support to: ECOBANK Bamenda Acc. No: 0040812604565101 **or** Carmel Cooperative Credit Union Ltd. Bamenda Acc. No: 261 **or** ORANGE Mobile Money: 699902618 **or** MTN Mobile Money: 674495895.

PUBLICATIONS BY CHRISTIAN RESTORATION NETWORK (CRN/PRAYER STORM)

1- Prayer Storm Daily Prayer Guide (monthly devotional)
2- Power Must Change Hands Vol.1: Dealing with Evil Foundations
3- Power Must Change Hands Vol.2: Pursue Overtake and Recover All
4- Power Must Change Hands Vol.3: Jesus Christ Must Reign
5- Power Must Change Hands Vol.4: Arise and Shine
6- Power Must Change Hands Vol.5: Family Restoration 1
7- Power Must Change Hands Vol.6: Family Restoration 2
8- Power Must Change Hands Vol.7: Raise an Altar
9- Power Must Change Hands Vol.8: Commanding Total Victory
10- Power Must Change Hands Vol.9: Enjoying Your Freedom in Christ
11- Power Must Change Hands Vol.10: Supernatural Breakthrough
12- Festival of Fire Series No.1: Let the Fire Fall
13- Festival of Fire Series No.2: Anointed Vessels
14- Festival of Fire Series No.3: God's Agent of Revival
15- Festival of Fire Series No.4: Raising Altars of Restoration
16- Festival of Fire Series No.5: Foundations of a Blessed Family
17- Dominion
18- Divine Overflow
19- Unbreakable
20- Higher Heights

21- Arresting Family Destroyers 1
22- Arresting Family Destroyers 2
23- Praying Like Jesus
24- Conquering the Giant Called Poverty
25- Generous Living
26- Bind the Strongman
27- Personal and Family Deliverance
28- A Difference by Fire
29- Your Time for Divine Expansion
30- Jesus Our Jubilee
31- The Choice of a Friend
32- Christians and Politics
33- A Dynamic Prayer Life
34- Restoring Broken Foundations

NB: Our publications are in English and French.

For copies, contact your local books store or direct your request to:

Prayer Storm Team
P.O. Box 5018 Nkwen, Bamenda
Tel.: (237) 679465717 or 675686005 or 677436964
crnprayerstorm@gmail.com
prayerstorm@christianrestorationnetwork.org

Prayer Storm Online Store:
With MTN or Orange Mobile Money *(for those in Cameroon)* and E-Wallet *(for those abroad)*, you can easily obtain the electronic version of this book and other CRN publications via **www.amazon.com** or via **www.amazon.com** at **https://shorturl.at/pqxyT** or **www.christianrestorationnetwork.org/our-bookstore**. **https://goo.gl/ktf3rT**

Contact (237) 679.46.57.17 or
prayerstorm@christianrestorationnetwork.org

www.ingramcontent.com/pod-product-compliance
Lightning Source LLC
LaVergne TN
LVHW050535100826
845148LV00002B/571

* 9 7 8 1 6 3 6 0 3 3 4 7 1 *